Patient or Profit
Where is the Love?

Adah F. Kennon, Ph.D.

Copyright © 2019 Adah F. Kennon, PhD.

All rights reserved. No part of this book may be reproduced or transmitted in any form or by any means, electronic or mechanical, including photocopying, recording or by any information storage and retrieval system, without permission in writing from the publisher.

Sheba Enterprises—Las Vegas, NV
ISBN: 978-0-578-54807-4
Library of Congress Control Number: 2019910985
Patient or Profit: Where is the Love? | Adah F. Kennon, PhD
Available Formats: eBook | Paperback distribution

skitldu@gmail.com
Sheba Enterprises
Printed in the United States of America

DEDICATION

This book is dedicated to all caregivers, and especially those who care for military veterans diagnosed with kidney disease and on dialysis. When all else fails, my best advice to you is to "keep it light," because the dark side is just too heavy.

CONTENTS

DEDICATION iii
FOREWORD ix
AUTHOR'S NOTE xi
PREFACE xiii
ACKNOWLEDGEMENTS xv
INTRODUCTION xvii

I. THE PATIENT

Chapter 1: A Place Called Home 1
Chapter 2: When Fantasy Becomes Reality 10
Chapter 3: Strong Foundations Make for a Good Beginning 16
Chapter 4: An Oath of Honor 18
Chapter 5: Good Karma Comes Back 20
Chapter 6: Great Expectations 21
Chapter 7: Calling All Healing Angels to the Floor 23
Chapter 8: The Shining Star... 25
Chapter 9: About Cholesterol, Triglycerides, Lipids
and Kidney Disease 27
Chapter 10: Statins 31
Chapter 11: Prior Authorization 32
Chapter 12: And the Winner is? 36
Chapter 13: Time Is Not On Your Side 39
Chapter 14: Fool's Paradise 41
Chapter 15: Gotcha 45

Chapter 16: My Body, My Choice 48
Chapter 17: The In-Crowd 52
Chapter 18: Health Outcomes Data and Clinical Trials 58
Chapter 19: Trial Group Participation – The FDA 61
Chapter 20: You've Got to Get What You Need 63
Chapter 21: Misuse and Abuse 66
Chapter 22: Just Below the Surface 68
Chapter 23: A Rose by Any Other Name 71
Chapter 24: It Starts at the Top 73
Chapter 25: The Devil is in the Details 77
Chapter 26: The Eye of the Hurricane 81

II. THE PROFIT

Chapter 27: What's in Your Chocolates? 84
Chapter 28: Wealth Defined 88
Chapter 29: The High Cost of Pacifiers 90
Chapter 30: Deal Breaker Aftershocks 93
Chapter 31: Coding is King 96
Chapter 32: What's for Dinner? 100
Chapter 33: True Colors Will Show 101
Chapter 34: Emissaries and Their Trappings 105
Chapter 35: The Power of Knowing 108
Chapter 36: Knowing or No-ing? That is the Question 110
Chapter 37: Fail to Plan, Plan to Fail 117
Chapter 38: Know the Current Situation 119

Chapter 39:	Count Your Blessings	122
Chapter 40:	The Shortest Distance Between Two Points	124
Chapter 41:	Will the Cavalry Come to Our Rescue?	126
Chapter 42:	If I Woulda- Shoulda- Coulda Club	129
Chapter 43:	Caregiver Reflections	131
Chapter 44:	The Way is Clear	132
Chapter 45:	Conclusion	135

EPILOGUE 136
REFERENCES 139
APPENDICES 141

FOREWORD

I can't help but wonder if politicians in the U.S. Government are traitors to certain military in the Army? My wife, Dr. Adah F. Kennon, has written this book based on our experiences dealing with her being my caregiver. The topic concerns how extremely difficult it has been for me to get the only prescription medicine that will treat my lipid health problem. Without it could mean death.

The specific concern deals with what the United States Health Industry calls the "prior authorization process," which appears to discriminate as to which patient can receive the lipid controlling medication. It is an injection given every other week and is quite expensive.

I am a WWII and Korean War veteran who retired honorably after serving 20 years active duty. Before enlisting in the Army, recruiters told me that if I served and retired honorably, the U.S. Government would pay for me and my dependant's health care for life, with no charge to me. The U. S. Government pays for some, but not all. In 2017, I paid close to $4,000 in health care costs, which the U.S. Government would not pay.

U. S. politicians broke this promise. They went to the Supreme Court which stated the government did not have to keep its promise, because we veterans were not given the promise in writing. To me, this is an unconscionable act, because we veterans of that era put our bodies and lives on the line, so that Americans would not be speaking German or Japanese.

Every time an American adult or child reads what is written on my Army retirement cap, they thank me for my service. It is difficult to except their thanks knowing what the U.S. Government did by violating their verbal contract to those of us promised "free healthcare for life if we served and retired honorably." The politicians and the U.S. Government are guilty of "bait and switch."

Dr. Walter (Walt) B. Hammond

AUTHOR'S NOTE

Walt (my husband) is an honorably retired military (Army) veteran. We are both of mixed (or multi) racial heritage (African American, Caucasian and American Indian). America is unique in that: (1) individuals having any African ancestry are considered as African Americans, and (2) Americans having two or more races are considered as multiracial. [1] While this book contains information for every caregiver and patient being cared for, special attention was given to historical and contemporary issues specific to African Americans and veterans. The terms "African American" and "mixed (or multi) race heritage (for example, African American/American Indian) are used interchangeably.

Please note that within the context of this book, the terms "prescription drugs, drugs, medications, prescription medications and pharmaceutical drugs" are used interchangeably as each refers to the same substance used to identify, treat and/or cure a medical issue.

What you are about to read is not conspiracy theory. Nothing is contrived, hypothetical or unwarranted. Any misrepresentation, if present, is unintentional. The protection of the confidentiality and privacy of medical professionals and government representatives assisting us was of utmost concern. Therefore, no reference is made to any personal information which might identify or compromise them in any way. I have intentionally redacted (blocked out) any such information appearing in correspondence included in the appendix of this book.

This book is a true story based upon factual, verifiable information. The only exceptions to this are when I make reference to: (1) residents living in my fantasy cities of Chaos (the "*no-ings*") and

Caring (the "*knowings*"), and (2) what I call *the Chaos Cohorts* (aka the *Alliance*).

Within the context of patients obtaining rightful access to certain pharmaceutical drugs requiring medical prescriptions, *the Chaos Cohorts* (aka the *Alliance*) refers to four powerful entities, uniting for the purpose of creating barriers in order to accomplish their self-serving goals. It is not hard to imagine that such entities or alliances actually exist, given everything that is happening in the United States today. While their descriptions are based upon profiles of real life organizations, this particular pseudonym is purely of my own creation. I do not know whether or not an alliance, group, agency, organization or coalition by this name actually exists, and any similarity to an entity actually bearing this name is merely coincidental.

PREFACE

When I started writing this book, my intention was simple. My goal was to help caregivers of patients, diagnosed with kidney disease and on dialysis, overcome barriers encountered during the prior authorization process when seeking approval for life saving pharmaceutical drugs requiring medical prescriptions. I wanted to share what happened to us, hoping that others could relate and benefit from our struggles.

As the book evolved, it became obvious that what I had initially labeled as the villain was actually just a carefully thought-out strategy being used by powerful entities (masquerading as our friends and benefactors) to accomplish their own self-serving goals. Uniting these entities in effect created an *Alliance*. I gave my creation its own identity, based upon the profiles of real life agencies and organizations. In doing so, it occurred to me that such an *Alliance* could indeed be possible in the real world.

The organizational structure of my *Alliance* was much like that of a tree. While there could be many branches, there was only one trunk. The branches received their sustenance through the trunk. As is true for a tree, the branches of my *Alliance* took their direction from one, very powerful and influential member. Together, they used this carefully thought-out strategy in ways geared toward making a dollar at our expense. They shared one goal - to satisfy their need for power, control and profit. They would go to any extent to get what they wanted.

Yes, they would even resort to legalized murder in the name of righteousness and patriotism. They were the lowest of the low, because they preyed on the most vulnerable and those who cared for them.

I began to wonder when it was that the focus of health care in this country turned away from being concerned about patients and towards big business profit margins. Who were these entities, how could they do this, and what kept us from recognizing their true agendas. Could they be stopped? If not, what could we do to protect ourselves and those in our care? What would be necessary to help us remain focused when faced with their tactics, so as to not lose sight of the real issues? How could we turn things around so that patients, once again, were the objects of this nations love, and not profit? *Patient or profit, where is the love?*

ACKNOWLEDGEMENTS

Writing this book called for skill, determination, clear focus, and humility. It also called for me to muster-up a lot of courage. First and foremost, I acknowledge and give thanks to my heavenly mother/father, God, and all emissaries of Divine Light (Michael, Gabriel, Uriel, Rafael, muse, ancestors), whose guidance, love, protection and patience with me made this project possible.

While I wish with all my heart that the circumstances had been different, I dedicate this book to my dear husband and twin-flame, Dr. Walter (Walt) Bernard Hammond. His passion for being of service to others by unconditionally sharing his vast storehouse of knowledge stands as a testament to him as a man of honor and integrity. His capacity to demonstrate unconditional care and concern for those around him who are in need has taught me the true meaning of Christianity. His resolve to overcome barriers encountered while fighting his own health issues has taught me how to be a survivor. His readiness to spit in the eye of danger and not be intimidated when he knows that he is in the right has taught me the meaning of courage. His many years of continued service to this country, and to the intended application of the principles upon which it was founded, has taught me the meaning of commitment to duty and honor.

I will forever be grateful to Walt for making the decision to allow me to participate as his caregiver in this current life-altering health journey. Being by his side as he fights his health challenges has allowed me the opportunity to be in the right place(s) at the right time(s) in order to gain insight into the world of kidney disease, dialysis, and what it takes to truly be of service to someone else. I only hope that I am able to learn from him and apply lessons learned, so that one day, I will develop the kind of character necessary to truly be a warrior.

INTRODUCTION

I am angry about this unexpected turn that our lives have taken. Why us? People say that we look younger than our ages. We live in Las Vegas, Nevada, the entertainment capitol of the world. We were going to travel, visit exotic lands, go casino hopping every day and eat out every night (see Appendix A for picture). What happened?

On a personal note, one of the great mysteries of life is how I ever got involved in this situation. After all, I was trained and practiced as a psychologist and counselor for many years. And believe me, there was more than enough happening on my job to be stressed-out about. I had hoped to get rid of a lot of negative energy following retirement and as I entered my golden years. As my husband pursued his business, I wanted my contribution to our relationship to be creating magical moments filed with fun and excitement. Being a high-energy person, I knew that it would almost take an act of Congress to get me to just sit around, watching the clouds go by and the grass growing.

I decided to start this cleansing by exploring a few items on my bucket list, especially in the areas of art and entertainment. Being able to take full advantage of my gym membership helped me realize a few personal goals like modeling fashion outfits and competing in body-building competitions. Making the cover of a well known fitness and nutrition magazine reassured me that all of the time and energy I invested had actually been for a reason. I started my own small business, and even produced and hosted a successful radio variety talk show. Then the unexpected happened. Everything was put on-hold due to a series of life-changing events, not of our own creation. Enter anger and frustration. First, I am angry at the medical world for making my husband the subject of experimentation and medical apathy. My husband has not smoked (past 54 years) nor had any alcohol beverage (past 11 years). Once a healthy and active person, he has undergone three failed knee replacement procedures, has kidney disease, and is now on hemodialysis (End Stage 5 Renal Failure). His kidney specialist (nephrologist) told him that decisions made by medical practitioners to inject him with contrast (intravenous) dyes during MRI procedures, in the name of efficiency, caused massive damage and the need for dialysis. Little remorse has been shown by those practitioners who have wronged him. Together, we made the decision for me to become his caregiver. I must say that my defense of him would put a mother lion, fiercely defending her cubs from harm, to shame. Second, I am angry with our government for sanctioning the use of barriers placed between my husband and access to a life-saving pharmaceutical drug requiring a medical prescription. Access to this drug might keep him from dying from an otherwise easily controllable condition.

The United States government did this by forming an alliance with a biopharmaceutical company, a drug distribution company (pharmacy benefit management company, PBM), and a health insurance company. They took a process, which was designed to help many people, and turned it into something no less than an instrument of evil. Their tactics were the use of deceit, deception, confusion, chaos and apathy.

What bothers me is the ease with which these entities were (and are) able to get away with this. I can't fault them entirely, because we as a society allow this to happen. Sometimes what they do is difficult to recognize, because their actions are falsely portrayed as decent and honorable mandates and laws. Sometimes they hide what they are doing behind sensational news items which are provocative and entertaining. In reality, these are distractions, or smokescreens with just enough factual information to make them believable. They want us to be preoccupied with the chaos and drama which accompanies these distractions. Their tactics are actually designed to keep us from raising our thoughts to a higher level, which is where they need to be in order to see beyond the deception. They do this so that they can pass laws and regulations which are created to serve their own agendas. They hope that we will not recognize or challenge them until it is too late to do anything to counter them. They count on us preferring to "bury our heads in the sand" rather than thinking that

there might be something that needs to be dealt with.
What are they hiding? What don't they want us to know? What is their true agenda? What can we do to keep from being used as pawns in their hateful games? Their goals are self-serving and do not include the improvement of the quality of our lives. Then again, there is nothing new about this. This has always been the agenda, especially of our government, when it comes to certain groups in this country, such as people of color and military veterans.

My husband is an 87- year- "young" Army veteran, who retired honorably after serving for 36 years – 20 with the U.S. Army (WWII Occupation and the Korean War; and,16 with Department of The Army as a civilian in the Pentagon and The Army Personnel Center). Are these entities trying to accomplish what two major wars, and a lot of living, couldn't make happen? Did they think that he (and others like him) wouldn't survive as long as he has?

There are dark days when I just get so angry and frustrated about what we are going through. I feel like there is a volcano inside of me that is ready to explode! Or, I feel so tired and depressed that it takes all of the energy that I have just to get through the day. It's true that feeling like I just can't take any more drama has become the norm for me.

There are many options already on the market which could provide assistance and make what we are going through a lot easier to deal with. Unfortunately, access to those resources is controlled by those who hunger for power and put a monetary price on sharing that knowledge. They don't care that their self-serving actions cause others to suffer. I sometimes wonder what it would be like to live in a world where helping people thrive by bettering health care conditions for everyone was actually a priority.

Yes, I am angry and frustrated about how the medical world and our government have failed to help my loved one. Yet, I refuse to become complacent, or to stop trying to discover reasons for why these things have happened. Each reason is like a piece of a puzzle – necessary to complete the whole and with a special place of its own. As a child, I enjoyed putting puzzles together, especially those forming beautiful pictures. I never thought that as an adult I would be faced with a real life jigsaw puzzle, especially one with such unpleasant images as what I was to discover.

I want to know the truth of it all. I know that knowledge is power. I also understand that knowledge is often accompanied by two things: (1) the possibility that you might not like what you discover; and, (2) a responsibility to do something worthwhile and positive with that knowledge in order to create change and help others (if they so choose) get to a higher level. I planned to follow-through with this responsibility, because I was not seeking membership in the if I "woulda- shoulda- coulda" club. I know that I have to be strong, because I now have both myself and my husband to care for. Everything not related to caring for him is on a "get to it when and if possible" status. I am at peace with this. My strength comes from God. My belief that we are not alone, and that there are others who can relate to our story, especially caregivers of kidney dialysis patients, is what sustains me in this quest.

If you are a military veteran, and especially of African American and/or American Indian heritage, then you may recognize and identify with much of what I'm going to share. After all, this government once called upon all male citizens of a certain age to become soldiers, expecting that a love for this country would motivate blind defense of the homeland, and obedience of orders, sometimes to the death. In return, your government promised you and your dependants, *free medical healthcare.*

My husband survived, paid the price, and is living a full life. He is a veteran. Due to life circumstances, he is now a patient and finds himself in medical need. He expects delivery and depends upon promises made to him so long ago by his government. Unfortunately, like so many others, he didn't get those promises in writing. Now he is being kicked to the curb. His government is apparently not interested in him or his problems. He is expendable. They deceived him, lied to him, and used him for their own purposes. Where is the love?

Despite his day-to-day battle with life-threatening health condition(s), my husband continues to show capable reasoning and decision-making skills. As his caregiver and advocate, I try to keep much of the stress that comes with everyday problem situations away from him. Deep down inside I know that what I am doing is a test of my true character and strength of spirit. I struggle to remain positive, because I am constantly fighting those battles which he does not need to bother with. Stress, for me, results from being faced with challenge after challenge. I get no time-off for vacations. We have people in our world who want to help us and offer their assistance. However, most of them can't be reached when things really get "interesting." After all, they have their own lives to live. I don't hold it against them, because even those with the best of intentions haven't walked a mile in my shoes. However, it makes it hard for me to trust them to do what needs to be done, especially in emergency situations. They haven't been trained in what to do as I have, and I don't have the time to instruct them. It's just easier to do it myself. After all, there is truth in the old saying that the road to hell is paved with good intentions.

On top of everything else, much resource information, while well-meaning, is at best, general in nature, and not specific to issues faced by caregivers of dialysis patients let alone caregivers having mixed race heritage. Walt encouraged me to find a way to channel my anger and frustration in a positive and productive direction. He suggested that I write a book. He thought that I might be good at it, seeing as how I have four advanced academic degrees, to include a Ph.D., along with over 30 years experience practicing in the areas of psychology and counseling. This sounded like a wonderful idea, and would give me something more to do than worry about him. I reminded Walt that as we are a team, I would write a book, but only if he would give input as a contributor. Walt has authored several books, and worked with individuals and groups of people, sharing information about a number of topics to include positive thinking and imaging. He has a military background which I lack. His input would be invaluable, because as a veteran he actually walked the walk and talked the talk.

Walt is my senior by 21 years. He has memories of what was happening in this country, especially for citizens of mixed race heritage, during the war years. He actually lived during that time period, and could tell the story as I certainly could not. Kidney disease and being on dialysis can really compromise your energy and ability to attend. Given this reality, there was no way that I was going to subject him to the stress that can accompany authoring a book. On the other hand, my experience as his caregiver more than qualified me to address those issues. With his agreement, we started one more journey, together.

Patients with kidney disease, who are also on hemodialysis, fight many battles in their war to survive. While there were many topics worthy of discussion, it was easy to pick the one which would become the focus of this book. The most important battle fought by us has been, and continues to be, how to overcome barriers encountered during the prior authorization process which prevent access to appropriate pharmaceutical drugs requiring medical prescriptions. The stakes are high and there is only one acceptable outcome. Winning depends upon giving everything that we have to fight this battle. With this in mind, the goals of this book are to help readers: (1) understand the nature of kidney disease, and some of the challenges faced by hemodialysis patients and their caregivers (especially patients and caregivers of mixed race heritage); (2) recognize who or what is more than likely controlling access to appropriate pharmaceutical drugs requiring medical prescriptions, how they do it, and how they benefit from it; (3) appreciate the wisdom of putting verbal promises in writing, because breaking them can have life altering consequences; and, (4) remain confident that it is possible to find ways to overcome barriers preventing legal access to these life saving prescription medications. The final section will offer additional recommendations, resources, and words of encouragement.

I used to try to hide my feelings of anger and frustration. After all, caregivers are supposed to be the strong ones. Aren't we supposed to keep a stiff upper lip, and smile through it all? After talking with other caregivers of kidney dialysis patients, I discovered that feelings of anger and frustration are not the enemy. In fact, it's healthy to experience these feelings, given all that we have to deal with, and what we watch those who we love and care for go through. I am convinced that the secret to survival as caregivers is to find healthy outlets through which these feeling can be expressed. It's what you do with feelings like these that counts.

Being a caregiver is a 24- hours a day, seven days a week commitment, which is why it's so important to develop effective survival coping strategies. I have learned that my ability to be an effective caregiver, and to make positive gains, depends
upon knowing how to sort through all of the information that is out there, so that I can get to what is reliable and relevant. I am constantly learning when to ask for help, as well as the right questions to ask. I ask a lot of questions, because much of what is happening in the world today doesn't make sense to me.

Walt and I have been together for thirty years. There have been many good times that we will treasure, and we pray that there will be many more to come. Believe me when I say that there has never been a dull moment, especially since he was diagnosed with kidney diseases and started hemodialysis. Each day brings new (and often unwanted) challenges to deal with. I am sure that every caregiver has a unique story to tell, along with words of wisdom to offer.

With this in mind, what you will read in the pages which follow represents a combination of information taken from research, my years of experience practicing as a psychologist and counselor in three states, and lessons learned during my time as a caregiver. Walt's contribution is based upon his experience in the Army (service and civilian), as well as information he acquired and management techniques he developed as the instructor and owner of his own business. Commentary is also included which should be considered strictly as our opinions, and may or may not be something that you agree with or can work with. You be the judge. You be the jury. If any of this brightens your day and lightens your load, then the purpose for writing this book has been accomplished.

CHAPTER 1
A Place Called Home

Once upon a time, in a land far away, lived two groups of people – the *no-ings* and the *knowings*. The *no-ings* lived in a city called Chaos and the *knowings* lived in a city called Caring. Both cities were located on an island with one great mountain called Olympus. The city of Chaos was on one side and the city of Caring was on the other side. The nearest inhabited body of land was called the Mainland. It was many miles away and difficult to reach.

Both cities were very special places. Three groups of people lived in each city. The majority of residents were called "patients," because they needed to take pharmaceutical drugs of one kind or another which required medical prescriptions. The other residents were their caregivers and their doctors/practitioners.

The *no-ings* were ruled by *the Chaos Cohorts*. *The Chaos Cohorts* were four powerful entities. They were the founding fathers of the city of Chaos; however, they did not live within the city limits. They lived in a suburban area, in close proximity to the city dwellers so that they could visit whenever they desired. *The Chaos Cohorts* were also known as *the Alliance*, because each entity was a power broker. Each one played a very special role in the life of a pharmaceutical drug.

The first entity was known as a *biopharmaceutical company*. It was responsible for making drugs falling into two categories – pharmaceutical drugs which required medical prescriptions, and drugs which did not require medical prescriptions (over- the-counter). The *biopharmaceutical company* determined how much each drug would cost. This entity had contacts on the island as well as on the Mainland.

The second entity was a *health insurance company*. Patients bought health insurance plans from this company, thinking that their medical expenses would be taken care of (or so they thought).

The third entity was called *the distributor*. This entity had a kind of split personality, because it was made-up of two components: a *wholesale drug distributor* and a *pharmacy benefit management company (PBM)*. The personality shown depended upon what task was required.

Both the *PBM* and the *wholesale drug distributor* employed sales representatives who also lived in the suburban area where the branches of *the Chaos Cohorts* resided. They went back and forth from the Mainland to the city of Chaos, delivering pharmaceutical drugs and over-the-counter drugs to the appropriate *distributors*. They had no contact with the patients or their caregivers living in the city; however, there were times when they were allowed to meet with the doctors/practitioners in order to entice them into purchasing merchandise favored by the *biopharmaceutical company*. Sometimes they even gave out free samples to sweeten the deal. Like the *biopharmaceutical company*, they wanted to make money in exchange for their services. When the free samples ran-out, the drugs were only available by sale. The sales representatives raised the initial prices set by the *biopharmaceutical company*, but ever so slightly so as not to bring attention to what they were up to.

The *pharmacy benefit management company (PBM)* was responsible for a number of things, including creating and taking care of the "formulary." The formulary was a list which included the name of each pharmaceutical drug, information about its purpose and other particulars. Over-the-counter drugs were not listed in the formulary. The city of Chaos kept its supply of drugs (both pharmaceutical and over-the-counter) under lock and key in a huge warehouse. Only the *PBM* and the *wholesale drug distributor* had access to this warehouse.

The fourth entity, which also had the most influence, was called the *federal government*. The job of the *federal government* was to oversee the other entities, very much as a bureaucracy would operate. It told the other entities what to do and how to do it, especially when it came to which patients would get access to the prescription medication.

The *federal government* had a very interesting relationship with both the *biopharmaceutical company* and the *health insurance company*. The *federal government* and the *biopharmaceutical company* were frequently seen together at social activities held in their suburban community. The *biopharmaceutical company* frequently picked-up bills for expensive event show tickets and when dining at fancy restaurants. It ensured its privileged position with the *federal government* by making substantial campaign contributions to chosen representatives.

The relationship between the *federal government* and the *health insurance company* was a little different. There were times when these two entities seemed at odds, competing for the same position of power, especially when it came to making final decisions regarding distribution of the drugs to patients. Then again, there were times when they got along, and even took turns when it came to making decisions. These instances were rare.

These *Alliance* members pretended to act in the best interest of the citizens of Chaos. In reality, they made-up their own criteria and used it to control access to drugs in both categories. They were especially tight-fisted when it came to who would get access to the pharmaceutical drugs. Access to drugs in this category was determined by criteria embedded into a process called "prior authorization." The prior authorization process called for a doctor/practitioner to complete a long and convoluted series of questions requiring very specific answers. Some questions were repeated, over and over again, required data and took a great deal of time and effort to compile.

This prior authorization process was initially designed as a way for people to improve their quality of life. It became a force of evil when *the Chaos Cohorts* used it to discriminate against groups of people. There was nothing fair about how *the Alliance* used this process. There was no rhyme or reason to it.

The Chaos Cohorts especially hated *no-ings* who were military veterans. Some of these veterans were members of minority groups, such as African Americans or American Indians. These veterans were not like the other patients. While they always returned home, their active duty commitments required that they leave the city and travel across the sea to the Mainland where they remained for short periods of time. Upon returning, they were among the few who were courageous enough to attempt to resist *the Chaos Cohorts*. They met secretly and in small groups. Options were explored and strategies were planned. None of them were successful. They couldn't create change, because their numbers were so few. They couldn't count on any support from the other *no-ings*, because everyone else either feared or admired *the Alliance*. These veterans were often discovered and punished. In fact, *the Chaos Cohorts* viewed them as rebels and actually tried to exterminate as many as possible. *The Alliance* was also suspicious of any doctor/practitioner or caregiver who treated or helped them. These entities did not respect the opinions of doctors/practitioners. Caregivers were tolerated, but not valued as essential.

The *no-ings*, as a group, were primitive and materialistic. They placed a high value on what they could see, hear, touch, taste and smell. These were also the things valued by *the Alliance*. So, it was a routine occurrence for them to offer materialistic things in an attempt to solicit favors from *the Alliance*. Some of the *no-ings* brought special gifts of money and food to members of *the Chaos Cohorts* as a way of trying to get what they wanted. Others tried to get special consideration from *Alliance* entities by saying and doing things that they thought would please them. Some patients just developed contacts with doctors/practitioners who knew how to work the prior authorization process to their advantage. The bottom line was that neither *the Alliance*, nor the *no-ings* (with the exception of the veterans) cared that some who wouldn't qualify for the prescription medication would die, needlessly and painfully. None of them gave a second thought to how desperately all of the patients in the city needed access to the prescription medication, or the unfairness of the selection criteria. Controlling access to the drugs, especially those pharmaceutical drugs requiring medical prescriptions, made *the Alliance* entities feel powerful. They just didn't care about anything except satisfying their own needs.

Anyone suspecting the true agenda of *the Alliance* kept their feelings to themselves. They feared that *the Chaos Cohorts* would target them and deny access to the drugs they so rightfully deserved. The only way that they could let-off steam and show resentment of their predicament was to take it out on each other. They treated each other with indifference and a lack of compassion. Questions were not tolerated. No one asked them. They all turned a blind eye to what was happening, followed decisions made by *the Alliance* and tried to survive as best they could.

Each day, the people of Chaos worked from sunrise to sunset, only to give their profits to *the Chaos Cohorts*. *The Alliance* wanted to take away everything that the residents had, to include their dignity as people. *The Alliance* demanded absolute obedience from the residents of Chaos. In fact, they demanded that they be worshiped by them, almost as if they were gods.

The four entities of *the Alliance* went so far as to pool their funds and bought a lighthouse that had a very tall tower attached to it. In that tower was the "light of all lights," that shined 24-hours each day, seven days per week. *The Chaos Cohorts* misrepresented the true nature of this light, claiming that it possessed special powers which could control everyone living in the city. With the exception of the veterans, all of the residents were mesmerized by the intensity of this light, which shined on them at all times. They believed what they were told by *the Alliance*. Little did they know that there was nothing in it that could really hurt them. Its only purpose was to draw attention away from what *the Alliance* was actually doing and to keep the residents submissive.

Using the "light of all lights" in this way proved to be the perfect distraction allowing *the Alliance* to carry out their own agenda. Numerous events played out while this light was shining which were characterized by confusion, drama, deception and apathy. This also kept the residents from asking too many questions about the prior authorization process. This had been going on for so long that everyone believed it to be normal. The consequence of this fear for the residents, which was a creation of their own minds, was that they settled for a life far less than they deserved.

One day, a patient who was a veteran of mixed race heritage decided to explore life on the other side of the mountain. Someone told him a story about a wonderful city called Caring. He found it hard to believe that such a place existed, because it was so different from what he knew. Being a veteran, he decided to attempt the journey.

Upon arriving in Caring, he couldn't believe what he found! He was so amazed that he stopped the first resident he met (who happened to be a patient) and asked him what was going on. Once the patient found out where the veteran traveler was from, he understood why he was confused by what he saw. He began to explain their philosophy of life, and how it differed from the one that the residents of Chaos had been indoctrinated with and encouraged to believe in. The patients living in Caring were called *knowings*. They were intelligent, wise and generally more evolved than the *no-ings*. The *knowings* were kindhearted, and showed concern for the welfare of each other. They were independent thinkers who took pride in their ability to ask questions and think outside of the box.

In contrast to *the Chaos Cohorts*, the citizens of Caring used their prior authorization process as it was originally intended - for the betterment of their people. Everyone in their city prospered. It was truly a wonderful place to live! The *knowings* approached problems logically, rather than with pure emotions or hidden agendas. Being able to make use of the skills of problem solving and strategic thinking were freedoms they treasured, as well as being able to do something positive about what they discovered. They were excited about the possibilities that might result from exploring options. The *knowings* understood that knowledge is power and treated that power with humility and respect.

There was no one ruler in the city of Caring. Final decisions regarding access to drugs, both pharmaceutical and over-the-counter, were made by a committee of the city's wisest and kindest elders (male and female). As was true for the *no-ings*, the residents of Caring kept their supply of drugs in a huge warehouse. They also maintained a formulary listing information about each one.

Patients requesting access to the drugs were given an opportunity to ask questions as well as to address the committee and voice their wishes. Opinions of doctors/practitioners were rarely challenged. These professionals were highly respected members of the community, and their comments were greatly valued. Every patient had access to drugs in each category, as long as their need was legitimate. Cases earmarked as "medical necessity, please expedite," were, of course given priority.

The veteran traveler from Chaos had no idea that the residents of Caring knew about life in Chaos. It was common knowledge that *the Chaos Cohorts* lusted for power, control, and profit. The residents of Caring also knew about "the light of all lights," and how *the Chaos Cohorts* used it. It could not reach them due to their location. In any event, they were not afraid of this light. They knew that it did not possess special powers, except what was given to it by the residents.

They would never be controlled by *the Alliance*, because they knew what these entities were really up to.

Jubilant about his discovery, the veteran traveler immediately requested permission to remain in Caring. The committee of the city's wisest and kindest elders (male and female) met to consider his request and determine the best course of action. After much deliberation, they decided to grant his request, but with three conditions. The first condition was that he was to return to Chaos and tell others what he discovered. The second condition was that he was to guide others back to Caring, but only if they really wanted to start a new life. The final condition was that he was to adopt the philosophy of life cherished by the patients in Caring. The veteran traveler agreed, and began the journey back to Chaos.

When the veteran traveler arrived in Chaos everyone wanted to know what he discovered. Being away from the city, even for a short time, had dimmed his memory of how intense the "light of all lights" was. He was never really mesmerized by it to begin with. The veteran traveler told everyone the truth as told to him by the residents of Caring. He told them how their false beliefs about the "light of all lights" allowed *the Alliance* to keep them in bondage. He told them about the philosophy of life valued by the *knowings*. But, most of all, he told them about how the residents of Caring used the prior authorization process to help everyone in their city "thrive."

The veteran traveler noticed that something very strange was happening to the residents of Chaos as he talked to them. They started asking him questions - all kinds of questions. They asked questions about the city of Caring and those who lived there. How did they know about them and what was going on in Chaos? What made them think that they could not be controlled by the "light of all lights?" They were intrigued by the possibility of being able to think outside of the box and be self-governing. Most of all, they wondered what it would feel like for all to have fair access to pharmaceutical drugs and over-the-counter drugs. What would it be like to "thrive?"

When the veteran traveler finished telling his story, just about everyone in Chaos wanted to move to Caring. There were a few who seemed undecided as to what to do. However, they also listened to what the veteran traveler had to say.

Time was of the essence. A rumor was going around the city that soon the sales representatives were going to stop giving-out free samples of the pharmaceutical drugs. *The Alliance* discovered what they were up to and directed them to stop. There was no profit in it for them. In the mean time, *the Chaos Cohorts* heard about his adventure. They tried to discredit the veteran traveler by calling him a traitor. Each attempt made by them to do this only served to increase his popularity with the residents. As fate would have it, a movement was being created by those who initially appeared undecided that would be the first step in the eventual undoing of *the Chaos Cohorts*.

The Chaos Cohorts realized that they were losing control. They couldn't allow anyone to leave Chaos. If everyone moved away, then there would be no one left for them to control. No one would be there to worship them. They decided to go to the light house and check the "light of all lights." Obviously, something was very wrong, and needed fixing, right away. Once there, they climbed the stairs to the top of the tower. In the distance, they saw long lines of patients, caregivers, and doctors/practitioners actually leaving the city of Chaos. *The Alliance* had no idea that their inability to keep this from happening was the second step sealing their eventual downfall.

To their astonishment, they saw the "light of all lights" grow dimmer and dimmer with the departure of each resident. It finally grew so dim that it was barely visible.

In a surprise move, the few residents who initially appeared undecided about the veteran traveler's story voted to remain in Chaos. They did so for a reason. The words of the traveler touched something deep within each one of them that they never knew existed or imagined possible. If others could live in an environment where they could thrive in this way, then it might also be possible for them to create something new and different without leaving their homeland. These *no-ings* knew that they would never be the same. In fact, they were becoming *know-ings*! Something within them had been set on fire. It might take time, but they decided to come together to create a plan that would once and for all end the reign of *the Chaos Cohorts*.

The *Alliance* was so preoccupied with the residents leaving the city that they forgot about those who remained. This proved to be a fatal mistake for them, because it allowed those who remained time to organize and plan a course of action that would forever end their reign. As they watched the procession, *the Chaos Cohorts* realized that soon they would no longer have a reason to exist. There would be no one left who wanted anything that they had to offer. There would be no one left to worship them. They knew that some day the "light of all lights" would go out forever. Like the Greek gods of Mt. Olympus, *the Chaos Cohorts* would eventually fade away.

CHAPTER 2
When Fantasy Becomes Reality

I'll admit that the story of the *no-ings* of Chaos and the *knowings* of Caring was one of my own creation. Then again, who is to say where fantasy ends and reality begins. The characters may change and the times may vary. The themes remain eternal and the consequences will be repeated unless different choices are made. As different as the settings are, there are many similarities between *the Chaos Cohorts* (aka *the Alliance*) and the major power brokers in America today, especially concerning legitimate access to prescription medication. Indeed, I submit that the preponderance of evidence suggests that America and the fantasy city of Chaos are one in the same. Consider the following.

It's 2017, and what does the typical 18- year -old American male (of any ethnicity, race or economic class) think about? The list is long and probably includes: girls, sex, fast cars, listening to popular music, having a good time, the internet, being "friended" on facebook, more girls and food. There is little doubt that they all pursue their mission with clarity, dedication and passion.

Now, flash back to the year 1948, when the social and economic climate in America was quite different than today. What were conditions like for people of mixed race heritage, as a group, in the United States? Well, there were some significant differences. History reflects that overt segregation, discrimination and racism were the laws of the land.

I wasn't around then, but Walt certainly was. He was old enough to realize what was happening, and his recollections are quite clear to this day. Times were perilous, especially for African Americans, and many battles were being fought on the home front. However, all 18 -year- old males of that era were most likely thinking about girls, sex, transistor radios, long-playing records, and baseball.

A popular weekend activity in 1948 for any member of that age group, regardless of ethnicity, race or economic class, was going to the movies. There they could watch (and maybe pretend to be like) romanticized versions of their favorite western cowboy stars or war heroes. Those were the only images of knights in shining armor available to African American males. Those movies reflected the existing societal values of the times, and were what the governing powers allowed to be shown.

Images projected through the media provided many opportunities to think about something else that could possibly be just around the corner for them –military confrontation with the Soviet Union as a consequence of increasing Cold War tension. They were probably wondering when their numbers would come up, because a military draft had been instituted in 1948 by Harry S. Truman, President of the United States.

What sort of a leader was President Truman? What was the character of this man? Given that people are influenced by the society in which they live, it is likely that he held views which were shaped by what was going on around him. President Truman was born in 1884 in Missouri, a state with a history of slavery. During that time period, any individual having any African ancestry was considered a black person. It did not matter that you were of mixed racial heritage. African Americans were treated as second-class citizens, segregation was the law of the land, and lynchings were all too common.

Walt's best recollection of President Truman was that early on in his political career he was not known for being especially concerned about the welfare of African Americans in this country. However, President Truman was certainly a very controversial figure. In fact, of all of the things he accomplished, Walt remembers President Truman for assisting with the creation of the United Nations in 1945, ordering the first atomic bombs to be dropped on Hiroshima and Nagasaki which brought an end to WWII in 1945, and issuing executive orders which marked the start of racial integration in military and federal agencies in 1948.

A lot of veterans will remember President Truman with mixed emotions, because of the consequences of a series of decisions he made during his two terms in office. The Korean War serves as an example.

Walt remembers this time period, because he was serving in Japan when the Korean War broke out. According to him, some people gave the President credit for ending the fighting in that area of the world. Others criticized him for the decisions he made, such as when he refused to send additional troop support or use atomic weapons during an engagement at the Yalu River.

Walt recalls that a million Chinese solders amassed on their side of that river, ready to attack United States troops. President Truman denied requests from one of his top military leaders, General Douglas MacArthur (a five-star general and field marshal of the Philippine Army) [2], for more support to fight that horde. His denial resulted in several American units being overrun and destroyed, to include practically the entire West Point graduating class of 1950.

No matter what was thought of President Truman, he was the president of the United States, and Commander- in- Chief of the Armed Forces, from 1945 to 1953. He was also expected to set the moral tone for the nation.

Now back to the year, 1948. Our government needed to exert more control over citizens than ever before, because the country needed cannon fodder. Walt was 18 years old when, on June 24, President Truman promoted and Congress approved the first peacetime draft system known as the Selective Service Act. Beginning on July 20, 1948, every male U.S. citizen between the ages of 18 and 26 was required to register for the draft.

There were few legitimate options for young African American males of that era who wanted to advance themselves financially and educationally. The powers in control created and sanctioned barriers in the name of segregation and discrimination. This limited access to opportunities leading to the better things that life had to offer. Walt remembers listening to radio programs and reading newspaper articles suggesting that this reality was even supported on some level by President Truman during the early years of his term.

African Americans who did not readily volunteer for military service were faced with powerful recruiting strategies developed and used by this government as extra enticement – promises of travel to exotic places, adventure, vocational training, educational opportunities, good food and free lodging. It's not hard to imagine that the promise of these incentives tricked many into believing that things would improve for them once the war was over. Enlisting in one of the branches of the armed forces offered the promise of prestige and security so often associated with government positions.

In addition to everything else, this was something that had the blessing of the moral leader of the country, the President of the United States. What could possibly be wrong with this picture?

African Americans celebrated all over the country on that day in 1948, when President Truman abolished racial segregation in the armed forces and federal government by executive order. Walt remembers hearing about it over the radio. Maybe President Truman did this to advance his own political career, but who cared. A change had come and the climate was one of anticipation. The reality was that it would take another two years before this executive order would become a law. In the meantime, only a few became officers. African Americans, while present, were primarily represented in the lower ranks.

How many of these young men really paid attention to the details included (or not included) in the legal contracts that they were entering into with this government when they enlisted, or requested copies of what they were signing? After all, they were probably preoccupied with all of the drama that accompanied those "typical " 18-year-old American male thoughts of 1948 – girls, sex, transistor radios, baseball, long playing records, and imitating the actions of movie idols and heroes.

Now comes the "light of all lights" – the lure of *free medical health care*. Walt was one of those 18-year-old African American male citizens (of mixed heritage) who voluntarily enlisted in the Army in 1948. The only criteria for enlistment, was that he could "dig a fox hole and shoot a gun." He would advance quickly because he could read, write, and had graduated from high school. Many of his Caucasian counterparts were functionally illiterate. Walt was to be paid seventy-five dollars per month. Twenty-five dollars of that amount would be taken out in the form of a savings bond. The remainder would be used for personal hygiene items, entertainment, and other expenses.

Like so many others, Walt set personal goals, as well as goals which would benefit the greater society. His personal goals were to advance himself educationally and economically. His pledge to America was to put his life on the line by defending this country's citizens, to defend the Constitution of the United States, and with the exception of unlawful orders, to obey mandates as issued by the most powerful representative of the government of this country, the

Commander-in-Chief of the Armed Forces, otherwise known as The President.

In return, one of the promises made to Walt by this government for his effort and sacrifice, was *free* medical- health -care for life for himself and his dependents, if he lived to retire honorably. Little did he realize that he was to become a victim of a "bait and switch" action. The dream of a better quality of life must have been quite an incentive for Walt, because in America, health care was sharply divided along racial lines.

Segregation for African Americans in the civilian arena was a reality that had gone on for generations. Laws and practices were put into place by this government which resulted in a denial of equal access to health care and forced the use of separate, inferior medical facilities. There is no doubt that this difference impacted the quality of medical care in every respect, and also made for a shorter life expectancy. This unequal treatment was justified as being a reflection of the social climate of the times, which labeled African Americans (and people of mixed race heritage in general) as being inferior to their Caucasian counterparts

With the passing of years, the fulfillment of Walt's dream has yet to be realized. The year is 2017, and he is a veteran. Decades of segregation, discrimination, racism, and a lack of access to appropriate health care have taken a toll on African Americans, as a group, in this country. Above average rates of chronic diseases to include kidney disease and heart disease, are a few of the sad legacies of this abuse. On a personal note, I can't help but notice that every time I go with Walt to his dialysis center, the overwhelming majority of patients are African Americans and/or people of mixed race.

As is true of any rebel, the fact that Walt is medically challenged has not dimmed his zest for life or his fighting spirit. He knows the face of the old, familiar enemy very well, because he has dealt with it all of his life. His story serves as a reality check for those who still believe that this country sees appropriate health care as a right due all citizens regardless of the ability to pay or the color of their skin. The general population of this country is now experiencing what it feels like when lies and deception are used by an external agent seeking to manipulate and control the quality of their health care. And, there is a new player to contend with - *medical apathy*. When it comes to acquiring legitimate access to pharmaceutical drugs requiring medical prescriptions, a deal has been made between health insurance companies, pharmacy benefit managers (PBM's), and biopharmaceutical companies. As was true for the patients in the fantasy city of Chaos, each of these entities represents a branch of what I call *the Chaos Cohorts*, taking orders from and being enabled by the U.S. Government. Using government mandates and strategies, like bullets fired from a gun, *the Chaos Cohorts* are trying to do to Walt (and many other veterans) what the passage of time and two world wars could not. Their attempt to deny Walt, an honorably retired veteran, access to a life-saving pharmaceutical drug is equivalent to attempted murder!

The passing of years has not changed the fact that Walt continues to get medical health care which is not entirely *free* nor *appropriate*. In fact, the situation worsens on a daily basis. Access to appropriate life-sustaining pharmaceutical drugs requiring medical prescriptions, is being increasingly restricted. Now, at the age of 87, Walt appreciates that the devil is in the details. He understands why it is so important to get things in writing, and the value of examining contracts from all sides before signing on the dotted line. He knows how to be ever-vigilant in order to recognize and reject lies and deception used to advance self-serving agendas of entities which don't have his needs in mind. The patients of the fantasy city of Caring would recognize Walt as being one of their own and welcome him with open arms.

While this might have the makings for a great movie plot, to a soldier (now veteran) it represents no less than a slap in the face. Lied to and betrayed by his own government, Walt realizes what the bottom line really is. No longer serving as a soldier, this veteran's mission has become one of doing whatever it takes to ensure his own survival and decent quality of life. Walt will not have to fight this battle alone, because his wife is now his comrade in arms. We will figure it out, together. As told through the eyes of his wife, twin flame, and caregiver: patient or profit…where is the love?

CHAPTER 3
Strong Foundations Make for a Good Beginning

A depression era baby, Walt was born in 1930. He was the second youngest of seven brothers and sisters. His baby brother died one day after his birth. His father worked for the U.S. Postal Service and died when Walt was not quite three years old. His mother never remarried.

Walt spent his early years growing up in Philadelphia, Pennsylvania and Camden, New Jersey. His mother taught him the value of responsibility and a strong work ethic. Walt always remembered her teachings, which would prove to be a powerful influence on him throughout his life.

Walt's father, Winston Purcell Hammond, worked for the Post Office. He died when Walt was three years old (see Appendix C for picture). Walt's mother, Edith, was a woman of many talents (see Appendix B for picture). She reared her children without any outside financial assistance, and even made a home for one of his older cousins. She owned her own business, worked as a beautician and was a motivational speaker. Edith was also a dressmaker and supervisor for the U.S. Military in the Philadelphia Quartermaster Depot, making uniforms for soldiers during World War II.

Edith was a renowned psychic in the Philadelphia and Camden, New Jersey areas during the 1920's through the 1980's. She was so well known that people from all walks of life called upon her for readings. Walt told me that she was very protective of her children. She put a ray of protection around each one to keep them from harm. This ray was designed to last a lifetime.

All of Walt's siblings went on to become successful as adults. As the years passed, he watched three of his older brothers during World War II (WW II) join branches of the armed forces: one in the Air Force, one in the Army and one in the Navy. Due to an accident early in life, his oldest brother was assigned to a unit at West Point known as "The Buffalo Soldiers." All three came home to Edith, their widowed mother.

CHAPTER 4:
An Oath of Honor

After graduating from high school, Walt joined the Army in October 1948 (see Appendix D for picture). He was one of those African American soldiers who took advantage of every opportunity for advancement. Walt served in the Army, and became a First Sergeant at 23-years of age (see Appendix E for picture). He held assignments in Germany, and was in Japan when the Korean War broke-out. Upon returning state-side, his mother, Edith, greeted him by proudly displaying a service flag hanging across the front porch of their family home, with a big "blue" star on it (see Appendix F for picture).

Walt had no intention of allowing the reality of racism, discrimination and segregation in the United States to keep him from pursuing his dreams. He went on to earn an Associate's Degree in Computer Science (1966), a Bachelor's Degree in Business Administration (1973), and a Doctor of Divinity Degree in Metaphysics (1993).

Overall, Walt served for thirty-six years, 20 years with the U.S. Army including WWII (Occupation, both in Japan and Germany), the Korean War, and 16 years with Department of The Army as a civilian in the Pentagon and The Army Personnel Center (retired as Master Specialist, MSP E-7 and GM 14). He not only served on active duty as a First Sergeant, but also worked as a personnel specialist, a computer programmer, analyst, supervisor, and manager in charge of The Army Officer Personnel Computer Systems, including promotions, assignment and various other systems.

While in the service, Walt served for two years on the Army Board to Correct Military Records (ABCMR), the highest Administrative Board in the Army. He was also the recipient of numerous awards through the Army, including a Presidential Certificate of Appreciation, Commander's Award, and Certificate of Appreciation, all of which were signed by General Officers.

CHAPTER 5:
Good Karma Comes Back

If there is any truth to the idea that experience, along with the choices we make in life, play roles in shaping who we become, then it is understandable that Walt has become the man that he is today. In other words, Walt has "good karma." He is just a really nice person who goes out of his way to help others. He especially loves giving time and resources to organizations supporting the needs of children.

Numerous Federal Government assignments as a manager and Equal Employment Opportunity (EEO) Representative, and assignment to the highest Board in the Army, provided Walt with experience in helping others who had no-where else to go, or no one else to turn to.

Walt's willingness to pass-on the knowledge gained from others motivated him to establish his own company, Development of Relaxation Powers, where he teaches self-hypnosis, positive thinking and imaging, home-budget managing and relaxation techniques within a holistic (mind, body, spirit) environment (see Appendices G and H for pictures). It might be difficult for some to realize that a man who was once a soldier can also be a poet. Walt has written poetry which appears in several publications, and is also a self-published author (see Appendix K for picture).[3]

Demonstrating care and concern for others earned Walt a nomination for the *Jefferson Award* in Nevada in 2010 for community service, along with being featured in a renowned magazine for professionals (see Appendices I and J for pictures).[4]

CHAPTER 6
Great Expectations

Walt is twenty-one years older than I am. Fortunately, father time has been kind to both of us. Both of us were in relatively good health when we moved to Las Vegas, Nevada in 1990 (see Appendices L and M for pictures). Of course, we were both beginning to face a few challenges generally related to the aging process, but nothing that we couldn't handle on our own, or with limited medical intervention.

Walt is a retired Army veteran and I am his dependant. Most of our health care needs were taken care of through resources at the local military (federal) hospital, run by the Department of Defense (DoD). Walt also had the option of going through the Veterans Administration system (VA), which is part of the Department of Veterans Affairs. The VA provides health care services to anyone who served on active duty in the armed forces, as long as they are honorably discharged.

I remember when things changed for Walt. The year was 2011. The Middle East crisis was happening, and he was "encouraged" to go off-base and into the civilian community for medical assistance and procedures. We had no idea that our introduction to *the Chaos Cohorts* was just around the corner.

As the years passed, we both developed additional health issues. With each new experience, we became more and more concerned about the quality of medical care and safety in both civilian and military hospitals. Our anxiety levels increased in direct proportion to hearing about things like the danger of "antibiotic resistant superbugs," and how poor, medical- team work and communication issues were resulting in greater numbers of patients dying unnecessarily. It seemed like we were always around people complaining that their doctors/practitioners were only trying to make money off of them, didn't really appear to listen to their concerns, or would move towards the door with the ending of a 15-minute session. Then, things really hit the fan when Walt's kidneys failed him and he had to go on hemodialysis, three times each week, four hours per session, at a center not far from our home. Walt did not cause this medical situation. It was initiated by a medical procedure performed by a doctor/practitioner.

CHAPTER 7
Calling All Healing Angels to the Floor

Life holds many mysteries. One of the greatest is what brings people from different walks of life together for a common purpose. Is it fate? Is it destiny? Is it having good karma? Is it divine intervention? Whatever the reason, we quickly discovered that having a healthcare team committed to working with us was a critical element in Walt's treatment plan.

After going through the usual list of less than adequate options, we were referred to a wonderful group of medical practitioners, and a great dialysis center which Walt currently attends (see Appendix N for picture). These healing angels welcomed us as team members from the first meeting, and communication was above average. Monthly meetings were held at the dialysis center, with the following participants: nephrologist, social worker, nutritionist, and lead nurse. Given everything that we were going through, we really appreciated their willingness to "go the extra mile" in order to ensure Walt's care and safety. The absence of medical apathy was quite refreshing.

In the beginning, I was unsure as to what my role as caregiver would be. That's why I was so appreciative of the patience shown by Walt's team members. It was true that I signed a lot of papers which formally appointed me as Walt's caregiver. But, honestly, I had no idea as to the nature of the commitment that I was making. I will forever be grateful for the respect and encouragement given to us by these angels, because it gave me time to develop a philosophy which would guide me as Walt's caregiver.

Early in our journey, and due to his kidney disease issues, it was obvious that the most important member of Walt's team would be his nephrologist. This is where having all of that good karma paid off, because Walt has one of the best specialists in practice. Just having good karma is not enough to keep the dark side totally at bay. Events which we were going to face during the weeks and months to come would test not only having good karma, but also the strength of the ray of protection placed around Walt by his mother. There are times when I find myself asking why the scales of life seem so unbalanced. It just seems so unfair that good people like Walt have to suffer more than others. Then, from somewhere deep inside of me, I hear a very soft voice answering my question by saying: "only God knows, it just happens."

I kid you not when I say that, next to God's mercy, the care and concern shown to Walt by his nephrologist, and his staff (you guys know who you are), has been responsible for saving his life (and my sanity). In the best of all worlds, this man should be permitted to formally act as Walt's primary care doctor/practitioner. However, we appreciate that he has a life of his own, along with other patients to care for.

CHAPTER 8
The Shining Star

Walt has a number of problematic medical issues. The one which most threatens his life is kidney failure. All of his doctors/practitioners considered, it is his nephrologist who has taken the leadership role in developing a plan which controls his symptoms and makes life bearable. He is the one who understands the importance of resolving as many of the other issues as possible which plague Walt, so that managing kidney issues can become the focal point. He is the one team member who is most involved in Walt's direct care. We respect and admire him for his capacity to "think outside of the box" in order to give his patients the best care available. This man would definitely hang his hat in the fantasy city of Caring.

The time and effort put in by his nephrologist more than justifies our total faith in his opinions and recommendations. If there is any justice in this world, the proven track record of his nephrologist should win him an automatic "pass" card in the pool of specialists deemed eligible by any regulatory agency or organization to make decisions and recommendations about what is appropriate and medically necessary for Walt's care, including appropriate prescription medications.

I believe that it's ridiculous that others who don't know Walt would dare to sit in judgment about the importance of any contribution made by his nephrologist, especially when it comes to managing factors which could adversely influence effectively treating his kidney disease. Serious consideration of his knowledge about Walt could be a life-saver.

Both Walt and I are doing all that we can to make this journey successful. We understand that this will require: (1) preserving his remaining kidney functioning; (2) effectively managing issues related to other medical conditions which are directly impacting his kidney functioning, and (3) gaining access to whatever the medical world can provide that will help him improve the overall quality of his life. We must do everything that we can to overcome roadblocks created by *the Chaos Cohorts*.

Walt appointed his doctor/practitioner (nephrologist) as his medical representative, because of his complete trust and faith in his decisions. We did not anticipate the consequences of this innocent action. Like the doctors/practitioners of the fantasy city of Caring, he was to be persecuted. His opinions were to be treated with indifference. Be that as it may, we all agreed that immediate attention should be given to addressing what could be done to control Walt's bad (LDL) cholesterol, lipids, and triglycerides. The technical part of my education as his caregiver was about to commence.

CHAPTER 9:
About Cholesterol, Triglycerides, Lipids and Kidney Disease

The next two chapters may seem to be unrelated to a discussion about how to overcome barriers encountered during the prior authorization process. However, my reason for doing so will become clear shortly.

One thing that I have found to be true is that a caregiver must do whatever it takes to be knowledgeable about any topic related to the medical condition of the one he/she cares for. This is important for three reasons: (1) to understand what is happening medically for your own personal growth and development, (2) to have meaningful conversations with team members, and (3) to know what you can personally do to be of assistance. The nature and range of topics will vary, depending upon the issues faced by those we care for.

As Walt's caregiver, I had to quickly access and digest a great deal of information, to include the impact of cholesterol, triglycerides, lipids and statins upon his remaining kidney functioning. I had to understand why his doctor/practitioner (nephrologist) was working so hard to help Walt get access to the only pharmaceutical drug designed to efficiently and quickly lower his bad LDL cholesterol. Because there was so much, I had to find a way to sift through everything so that I could narrow the scope of what I needed to know. This is when I started to understand the importance of trusting my gut feelings and intuition. I did not fully realize it, but things were in motion that would guide me to what I needed to learn. I was literally being pulled in directions that I had never experienced before. There were things that I needed to learn to assist Walt in the here- and- now. There were also things that I needed to learn in order to deal with a future action that *the Chaos Cohorts* would take against Walt. I could either dismiss this feeling, or go with it. I'll give you one guess as to what I chose to do!

What strategy would I use? I read specific articles, talked with Walt's nutritionist about diet restrictions, and reviewed as many of his lipid panel- lab results with his doctor/practitioner (nephrologist) as possible. I listened carefully to everything that his doctors/practitioners told me (especially his nephrologist) and took pages of notes for later reference. I needed to acquaint myself with the terminology used and expectations concerning acceptable and unacceptable findings. I also learned a great deal about how I could manage Walt's diet at home, which was a critical component of his treatment plan. Based upon all of the above, I was able to come to the following conclusions.

Cholesterol is a waxy substance. Our bodies make this, and it circulates in our blood by attaching to proteins known as lipoproteins. There are two forms of cholesterol: LDL (low density lipoprotein, bad cholesterol) and HDL (high density lipoproteins, good cholesterol).

Cholesterol can be good or bad for us, depending upon what it does in our bodies. HDL is a good form of cholesterol, and is responsible for tasks like making Vitamin D (for example, to absorb calcium and promote bone growth), and bile so that we can digest food. Terrible things can happen to us when we have too much bad LDL cholesterol, because it can lead to heart and cardiovascular disease and strokes.

Some of our cholesterol comes from the food we eat. That is why it's so important to know what foods a kidney dialysis patient can safely eat and what to avoid. Working with the nutritionist on Walt's team really helped me in this respect.

The liver is an important organ, because this is where most cholesterol is made. If the liver is not functioning correctly, then the bad LDL cholesterol can't be removed from the blood without assistance. Too much bad LDL cholesterol can cause coronary heart disease and heart attacks. Heart disease is common in people with chronic kidney disease (CKD). Hypertension is a major risk factor for coronary heart disease. In fact, many (if not all) of the patients on hemodialysis at the center that Walt attends are diagnosed with hypertension. Walt's liver can't effectively remove this bad LDL cholesterol from his blood. This is a life-threatening situation, because it directly impacts his kidney functioning.

The liver also makes something called triglycerides. Triglycerides are the most common type of fat (know as lipids) in the body. Triglycerides (lipids) are stored in fat cells, and are made of calories from the food you eat that are not used right away by your body.

Hormones help to release lipids, for example, when you need energy between meals.

The difference between triglycerides and cholesterol can be confusing. Both are found in the blood and both are a kind of fat (lipid). But, they are different kinds of fats. There are some hormones, for example, that use cholesterol to make cells. Triglycerides store excess calories and also supply energy. You may have high triglycerides, for example, if you normally eat a lot of deserts, then sit around and don't work off the extra calories.

Walt's condition is further complicated because his triglycerides are elevated. An elevated triglyceride level, along with raised bad LDL cholesterol levels, increases his risk of heart attack and/or stroke.

It's worth mentioning again that people with chronic kidney disease are at a higher risk of developing (or may already have) cardiovascular disease. If bad LDL cholesterol builds up in the arteries, it can make plaque, and develop into atherosclerosis (narrowing and hardening of the arteries). This plaque can clog arteries in the kidneys, which can cause this organ to shut down.

Having too much bad LDL cholesterol in your blood can also be caused by genetic disorders. An example of one inherited genetic disorder is Familial Hypercholesterolaemia (FH). This disorder can happen when your level of bad LDL cholesterol is too high, and can affect your body's ability to manage cholesterol.

There are two forms of Familial Hypercholesterolaemia (FH). Both are inherited from your parents. Heterozygous Familial Hypercholesterolemia (HeFH) is when you have one FH gene and one normal gene, and results when only one of your parents has FH. Your bad LDL cholesterol will be very high (above 190 for adults or above 160 for children), and you will have a family history of high cholesterol, heart disease or stroke.

Homozygous Familial Hypercholesterolemia (HoFH) is when you have two FH genes and results when both of your parents have it.

When it comes to having high LDL (bad) cholesterol levels, blood pressure, poor diet and lack of exercise are just a few of the risk factors of concern for anyone in the general population. Sometimes there are factors which you can't control, like your family history. Sometimes it's possible to control or prevent the impact of these risk factors by making lifestyle changes, or with lipid lowering prescription medications.

CHAPTER 10
Statins

Anyone watching television today probably knows that statin medications are used to lower cholesterol, which can reduce the risk of having a heart attack or a stroke. These medications stop the liver from making lipids, and thereby reduce fats in the blood. There are side-effects associated with all prescription drug medications, to include statins. While he has tried statins in the past, Walt can't take them because they cause him severe muscle pain and weakness.

As it concerns the impact of cholesterol upon his kidney functioning, Walt's doctor/practitioner (nephrologist) is the one person who best knows his total medical history, knows that he has made a "good faith" effort and failed when trying statins, and knows when it's time to move on to something that actually works.

Today there is a growing concern that some doctors/practitioners give-in and write prescriptions for specific high-priced and/or brand name drugs based upon patient demand. This has, unfortunately, influenced popular opinion so much, that many believe this to be a standard operational practice for all or most patients and doctors/practitioners.

While this may or may not be happening for some, let's be clear about this particular situation. Walt's doctor/practitioner (nephrologist) told him about a life-saving pharmaceutical drug. Walt did not ask his doctor/practitioner for a specific drug, let alone one by name. There is no doubt that Walt's desire to fight and live a good quality of life played a significant role in the decision made by his nephrologist to formally prescribe this pharmaceutical drug. This is the only option available to address Walt's medical need. Without it, he is at high risk for a heart attack and/or a stroke. He might die from something that could easily be controlled. If you were in Walt's shoes, what would you want your doctor/practitioner to do for you?

CHAPTER 11:
Prior Authorization

I have found that there are three characteristics which all soldiers (veterans, in Walt's case) seem to have in common. As a group, they are extremely goal oriented, focused, and always prepared to deal with unknown situations. If they have wives or significant others, then I would bet that these veterans are not shy about "laying down the law" to them when they don't follow suit!

I like to think that I already possess these characteristics. As my husband's caregiver, I'll be the first to admit that taking time to highlight and sharpen them has come in handy. Doing so helps me deal with the challenges and drama often associated with caring for someone with kidney disease and on hemodialysis.

I mentioned earlier that being an effective caregiver depends upon asking questions and making use of critical thinking skills in order to target relevant and reliable information. I also mentioned that there is wisdom in trusting intuitive "gut" feelings. In my case, the intuitive feeling concerned targeting and digesting the right kind of critical information in the least amount of time possible. As it turned out, this intuitive feeling was right on target. *The Chaos Cohorts* had either already made or were about to make decisions which, if unchallenged, could have life or death consequences for Walt.

An attempt was going to be made by *the Chaos Cohorts* to keep Walt, a veteran of mixed race, from getting access to the only pharmaceutical drug needed to manage a medical condition directly impacting his kidney function. The strategy which they were going to use would employ a process known as prior authorization. *The Chaos Cohorts* were going to use arguments to justify denial of access to the requested drug. They were going to claim that bits and pieces of the larger picture had not been collected thoroughly enough, long enough, timely enough or consistently enough. All of this was to be done with a complete disregard for the immediate need to address the condition of Walt's bad LDL cholesterol, lipids and triglycerides. They were going to demand the use of an inappropriate or weaker form of a statin medication before giving access to a more expensive and appropriate medication. They were going to disregard the fact that Walt had already tried statins and experienced severe side effects. The attack was to be systematic, relentless, and drain our energy reserves. What they were doing was just, plain, wrong! As his caregiver, it was my choice to put myself into the direct line of fire in order to do everything in my power to help him withstand this onslaught.

As is true for many, Walt has health insurance. In fact, he has two American Federal Health Insurances. He also has accounts with two pharmacies. Walt gets most of the pharmaceutical drugs which require medical prescriptions (and over-the-counter drugs) that he needs right away from a pharmacy located in a nearby community store. He also has an insurance policy through a company which processes on-going prescription medical pharmaceutical claims, and provides home-delivery for its members using a network of retail pharmacies.

Over the years, Walt's nephrologist has successfully submitted many medical prescription requests on his behalf. None of them have ever been questioned or rejected. As a competent, capable, and well-respected professional, his nephrologist has evaluated Walt and knows the reason why he orders medications. So, there was no need to anticipate any problems from Walt's community pharmacy when his nephrologist submitted a request for the "one and only" pharmaceutical drug able to control Walt's bad LDL cholesterol.

Needless to say, everyone was shocked when the community pharmacy denied his doctor/practitioner's request. Why was this happening? It had never happened before? We finally figured it out. The community pharmacy takes orders from *the Chaos Cohorts*. The pharmacist who denied the prescription request said that a requirement known as "prior authorization" had not been satisfied. Walt's doctor/practitioner (nephrologist) had the freedom to prescribe this drug. However, he needed to get permission from Walt's health insurance company before sending it to the pharmacy. If this approval was refused, then Walt might have to pay all of the fees himself, or be denied the medication, altogether.

Now, believe me when I tell you that I want to ensure the safety of any drug I take, or give to my husband. I do believe that the basic rationale for requiring prior authorization makes sense. I question <u>how</u> and <u>why</u> *the Chaos Cohorts* are allowed to abuse this strategy to advance their own power, control, and profit motive.

There are some positives about prior authorization which deserve mentioning. The basic rationale for needing prior authorization is to make sure that health insurance plan members: (1) get pharmaceutical drugs requiring medical prescriptions that are safe, effective for their condition, and cost-effective, and (2) confirm that the drugs qualify for coverage under the terms of the pharmacy benefit plan.

The prior authorization process can be used for purposes which differ from those it was originally intended. Entities forming the alliance known as *the Chaos Cohorts* are prime candidates for doing this, especially when they use it to create barriers between patients and access to appropriate life saving pharmaceutical drugs. One of the entities known as a health insurance company could easily lead this attack. Seeing as how this entity is one branch of *the Chaos Cohorts*, this wouldn't be so hard to imagine. Health insurance companies are primarily concerned with their own bottom line, which is to save money.

As one branch of *the Chaos Cohorts*, the health insurance company plays the leading role when it comes to using the process of prior authorization to determine access to and payment for pharmaceutical drugs requiring medical prescriptions. This entity can also use this process for the purpose of engaging in a kind of discrimination. Those patients who don't fit the qualifying criteria, as specified by them, are denied approval.

Walt's nephrologist has been working for over one year to obtain authorization for the one and only drug which will control his bad LDL cholesterol. It is easy to see how dealing with the bureaucracy associated with this prior authorization process could cause some doctors/practitioners to become discouraged and attempt to "opt-out" of a situation like this, especially when their time and effort goes unrewarded. Then again, Walt's nephrologist seems to have a backbone forged in steel. I'm sure that he would be the first to agree that the assistance of his dedicated staff proved indispensible in providing the hands-on time (for example, typing and research) required to complete all of the required paperwork involved in the process. There has been no resolution as of the writing of this book.

CHAPTER 12
And the Winner is?

Having a "to-do" list is an essential strategy which has served me well as a caregiver. It's challenging to meet my needs, as well as those of my husband, on a daily basis. Being able to think strategically is a must, as well as developing and using good time management and organizational skills. Appointments, for example, are recorded on a calendar as they are booked. Medical information (lab reports, copies of blood tests, summary notes from doctor's visits, and emergency information) is filed as soon as possible after being received. These items are kept in a location that's easy to get to. Lists of essential food items, along with expiration dates and medications are kept up-to-date and housed on closet shelves reserved exclusively for Walt.

It's hard to imagine how a business owner, like a doctor/practitioner, would be able to function successfully without knowing how to use time management and organizational skills. Being able to think strategically would be like icing on a cake. Just completing the paperwork involved in the prior authorization process calls for a doctor/practitioner to spend a great deal of time per patient. I can see how having a handle on these skills would be of benefit.

A doctor's/practitioner's ability to "think outside of the box" might ensure that a prior authorization request is approved when initially submitted with no appeal action involved. One strategy might be to start a patient on a free sample of a pharmaceutical drug, and then chart progress findings. Hopefully, the patient gets better. The doctor/practitioner could then present those findings to the health insurance company to justify a need for authorization approval, on the grounds that stopping the drug might hurt the patient in some way. A very good plan, indeed.

Since Walt does not have a medical prescription for the drug he so desperately needs at this time, the only way that he has been able to control his bad LDL cholesterol is by getting free samples from his doctors/practitioners. At this point, one might ask why a doctor/practitioner would go out on a limb like this to do something which might be seen as a violation of prior authorization and put his/her license in jeopardy. I like to think that it's because righteous people keep moving forward, especially when told to do something which contradicts the moral foundation upon which their profession is built. These doctors/practitioners would be welcomed as residents of the fantasy city of Caring, because they understand that the needs of patients aren't always the same as those of *the Chaos Cohorts*.

An unanticipated result of getting these free samples was that we were able to keep track of how well this free pharmaceutical drug was able to control and/or reduce Walt's bad LDL. In the mean time, Walt's doctor/practitioner (nephrologist, his designated representative) officially started the prior authorization process.

Walt and I were able to get copies of information submitted to the health insurance company by his doctor/practitioner (nephrologist). The first things that impressed us were the amount of information collected, as well as the number of times that questions were repeated.

The information required during the completion of the section entitled, "clinical assessment" serves as a good example of this. Walt's doctor/practitioner had to respond to numerous in-depth questions, such as: patient background and comprehensive health history; patient age; diagnosis; listing of all medications currently being taken, along with dosage; projected outcome about the possibility of substituting a generic drug which costs less than its brand-name counterpart; and, if the situation really represented a medical necessity.

As I reviewed this information, I became increasingly concerned that an entity known as a health insurance company felt entitled to tell a professional medical doctor/practitioner what to do in this manner? Why would anyone want to put barriers in front of a professional medical doctor/practitioner who was so passionate about demonstrating his/her humanity and doing the right thing, that he/she would add to an already lengthy "to-do" list by acting as an advocate or representative for his/her patient? The answer was clear, yet unconscionable. The bottom line for the health insurance company was "money," whereas the bottom line for the doctor/practitioner was "what's good for the patient." These opposites do not attract.

I can only imagine how a doctor/practitioner would feel if, after all of the planning and documenting, the health insurance company decided to stop the process. This could happen during any point in the process, and for any of the following reasons.

CHAPTER 13
Time is Not on Your Side

Reason for denial: The Time Expired "Merry-Go-Round"

When you pay for any kind of health insurance plan, the first step is that a contract is reviewed, agreed upon, and signed. This process usually represents a meeting-of-minds between you (the insured) and the health insurance company (the payer). In the case of health matters, the insurance document that you, the patient (insured) receive is commonly referred to as a health care insurance policy. This policy addresses a variety of areas, to include what must happen in order for things to kick-in, as well as financial consequences.

According to the health insurance company, failure to file forms on time is grounds for denial of the prior authorization request. On the one hand, I can appreciate the wisdom of setting time limit deadlines when it comes to filing forms, because there must be a great deal of paperwork involved in each case. It makes sense to have rules in place to move things along so as not to create a backlog.

Who sets the rules when it comes to health insurance policies? Certainly it's not the patient. Deadlines regarding the filing of forms can range from a few days to a few months. Every contract that we have received from an entity like a health insurance company has been pre-printed, and only reflects the position of the company. There is nothing mutual about it. It is the patient's (or a representative's) responsibility to be aware of the details. I have not experienced any extraordinary attempts on the part of the company to send out reminders. You can either go along with it, or find another company.

You might ask for an extension of the deadlines due to unforeseen circumstances. I wish you luck. A violation of the time for filing was cited as one reason for denial of Walt's prior authorization appeal request, even though his representative indicated (in writing) that he never received notification in the first place. No exception was made for this glaring extenuating circumstance (see Appendix S, Letter dated July 11, 2017). The details of what happened are as follow.

As his appointed representative, Walt's doctor/practitioner (nephrologist) made every effort to keep us informed about any communications received from the health insurance company related to the prior authorization process. Written correspondence would go back and forth, with the health insurance company sometimes sending letters to us or to the doctor/practitioner. Information contained in those communications often differed, depending upon who it was being sent to. So, whenever we received letters from the health insurance company, we made sure to forward copies to his doctor/practitioner, and vice-versa.

Walt's initial request for access to the pharmaceutical drug was denied; therefore, an appeal was initiated (see Appendix P, Letter dated March 8, 2017). Letters went back and forth; however, our assumption was that the originals were sent to the doctor/practitioner. The reason for this assumption was that the doctor/practitioner was Walt's representative. We had no idea that the doctor/practitioner never received the original notification from the health insurance company.

After a while, the health insurance company sent a letter directly to Walt, stating that the deadline to file an appeal had expired. We immediately called the doctor/practitioner who informed us that he never received notification from the health insurance company. The doctor/practitioner immediately notified the health insurance company about this, and requested an extension. The health insurance company denied the request, stating that the case had already been closed, and that a new case had to be opened. The new case would have to include another authorization letter from Walt appointing the same doctor/practitioner as representative. At that point, we had been working to get this pharmaceutical drug for almost one-year. The doctor/practitioner had already submitted all of the paperwork in the first go-round, to include three separate letters emphasizing medical necessity.

CHAPTER 14
Fool's Paradise

<u>Reason for denial: The patient took a relatively low-dose of a medication, or combination of medications, favored by the health insurance company. The patient stopped due to adverse side effects. The health insurance company required the patient to resume taking the medication, or combination of medications, as a preliminary step, and at a certain dosage, before confirming that this was not going to work. The patient, fearing a more severe reaction, would not comply. The health insurance company would not approve coverage due to noncompliance.</u>

Even if we are in the best of health, how many of us really take the time, or make the effort, to read all of the information written on the inserts stuffed into those boxes that medications come in? I'll have to admit that I don't always do this, especially if I am not feeling well. When I do, the first thing that I look for is a listing of the potential side effects. I like to think of myself as being a rational and reasonably informed person. For the sake of argument, assume that I am a patient faced with the following dilemma: either I take a drug favored by a health insurance company, at a dosage of their choosing, or I won't get prior authorization approval for access to the correct prescription medication actually needed. I would probably use the following decision-making process.

I know that all drugs (prescription, over-the-counter, and herbal formulations) have some kind of side effect. If logically I know that taking a drug might result in my experiencing a debilitating or dangerous side effect, then what could possibly motivate me to engage in delusional thinking to justify my taking that drug? Why would I risk my health and/or life by disregarding factual knowledge? Why would I take an inappropriate drug under any circumstance?

Let's say for the sake of argument that I comply. I consider the advice of my doctor/practitioner, a person who has my best interest at heart, and understands that all medications (prescription, non-prescription, and herbal formulations) have side effects. I assume that my doctor/practitioner considers the pros and cons of these side effects before recommending a course of action for me, and believes that the benefits outweigh the dangers. I know that, unless an emergency situation exists, I control what the final decision will be. After all, it is <u>my</u> health that is at stake.

Desperate people will often act out of that desperation. If I'm really desperate to achieve a goal (for example, prior authorization approval to obtain a legitimate medication prescription), then I might find a way to disregard the possibility of unpleasant consequences happening. I might even talk myself into believing that unpleasant consequences will <u>never</u> happen to me. My common sense and survival instinct goes out of the window. I don't feel well. I'm tired and short on patience. I decide to comply. I take a drug (which I know might hurt me), at the dosage required by the health insurance company, and risk experiencing problematic side effects in an attempt to do what the health insurance company (one branch of *the Chaos Cohorts*) says that I need to do in order to qualify for the drug that I know will really help me. I am motivated to do this by the thought of what life might be like for me if my survival depended upon access to a few free samples left by a drug company representative during random visits with my doctor/practitioner. What happens when the samples run out, or if the representative goes on vacation? What if the free samples are discontinued, because the powers that be fail to see a profit in giving them out? The best of all worlds, after all, is to qualify for a "legitimate" prescription. For that, prior authorization approval from the health insurance company is mandatory. I'll do what they say, and risk being hurt in the process.

The Chaos Cohorts are hard at work. They are masters when it comes to figuring-out what a person might do if his/her back is pushed against a wall. The tactics they use to persuade a person to comply with their mandates are enough to reverse the most resolute mindset of an otherwise logical, rational individual. They truly operate in the spirit of the "founding fathers" of the fantasy city called Chaos.

It doesn't take long for a patient in this country to figure out that doctors/practitioners generally start by prescribing less expensive (or sometimes weaker) forms of drugs, and then confirm that they don't work before moving on to drugs that are more expensive. This seems to be a standard practice, regardless of a patient's condition or ability to endure a drug. Maybe the doctor/practitioner wants to pursue a different course of action; however, this strategy, known as *STEP* Theory, is the one that health insurance companies require a patient to go through.

Again, the focus is on cost-effective care, in contrast to initially doing what needs to be done in order to meet the needs of the patient. This benefits the health insurance company. The authority of this branch of *the Chaos Cohorts* is empowered, while that of the doctor/practitioner is diminished.

In Walt's case, why on earth would he risk the consequences of taking a statin drug (for example, intense muscle pain and debilitating weakness)? He knows that adverse side effects will happen to him, because he has experienced them (see Appendices O and R). Thankfully, he has an ethical doctor/practitioner (nephrologist) who did not go along with this option. Kudos go out to Walt's doctor/practitioner (nephrologist), to Walt having "good karma," and to the ray of protection placed around him by his mother to keep him from harm! There is nothing new about this tactic. No one should be surprised that it's used. The branches of *the Chaos Cohorts* have employed it for many years, especially when dealing with certain segments of the population, like people of mixed race heritage.

Before the advent of television, many adults would entertain themselves by gossiping about current local and national events. Children were usually not included in these interactions; but, that didn't stop them from listening. It was in this way that Walt, then just a youngster, started hearing about the infamous Tuskegee Experiments taking place in Macon County, Alabama. That was back in 1932. With the passing of years, and as he grew older, Walt recalls understanding the nature of these unspeakable events, which took place for more than 40 years. This is his recollection.

The U.S. Public Health Service was running a study involving hundreds of poor African American men, primarily sharecroppers, who didn't know that they had syphilis, a sexually transmitted infection. Doctors/practitioners from the U.S. Public Health Service told them that something was wrong with their blood, and gave them placebos (for example, aspirin and mineral supplements). This travesty was continued, even after the disease became treatable with penicillin in the 1940s. Ineffective care was continued, in an attempt to track the full course of the disease. These poor men experienced much suffering and pain, to include blindness, insanity, and eventually death.

Why would anyone participate in such a study as this? A number of reasons come to mind. Advertising for the study was misleading. Certainly the researchers were deceptive about the true nature of the study, and did not inform participants about the entire purpose of the research or the dangers involved. It might have also been because the participants just trusted the researchers to do the right thing. After all, they were *government* "United States Public Health Service" representatives. And, they promised access to *free medical care*. Sound familiar? This proved to be a fatal mistake.

Chapter 15
Gotcha

<u>Reason for denial: The patient decided to take a medication or medications favored by the health insurance company, and endured problematic side effects. The health insurance company required that bad LDL cholesterol levels fall into a range which they specified, and for a "specified" time period. The patient's levels did not fall within this specified range for the specified time period. The health insurance company would not approve coverage.</u>

Generally speaking, it's important for all of us to keep up with our cholesterol levels, especially the bad LDL levels. Developing an informal or formal way of collecting, organizing, and presenting medical health history information can go a long way in your favor, especially in the event that you need to appeal a prior authorization denial.

It is important to cover all bases, just in case your request is denied. Collecting information which is reliable and accurate adds credibility to an appeal, and can build support for your argument(s). A useful strategy for me has been to record selected information from each of Walt's lipid panel profile print-outs in a notebook. Entries are kept in chronological order. I also include information about anything else that might have influenced the findings, such as a change in diet or medications.

Walt has been getting his cholesterol levels checked for so long that we have gotten used to the process. The determination of whether or not you have bad LDL cholesterol (low-density lipoprotein cholesterol) is made using these tests. Test results are used to predict risk for developing heart disease, and for treatment decisions and effectiveness.

Cholesterol levels may be periodically checked to see if the treatment plan (for example, medications) is working. It can take months between repeated cholesterol screenings, so be prepared. Remember that a prior authorization request can be denied on the grounds that sufficient information has not been provided to establish coverage of the requested medication.

I fail to understand how anyone can justify taking what might well be an inappropriate medication, for a specified time period, just for the sake of saying that you tried it. Why should a health insurance company dictate what you should or should not do in this type of situation? On top of everything else, what if it doesn't work? Was it worth the risk? Having said all of this, consider the following. The ability to collect this information in the first place calls for a patient to be subjected to a medication or medications, for a period of time specified by a health insurance company (a branch of *the Chaos Cohorts*). This may or may not result in the creation of new problems which will need to be addressed. Further, there is no guarantee that this will be beneficial. By the time that you get through, your body chemistry may really be in shambles!

What if you decide to go out on a limb and put your health at risk by taking medication which is at best "incorrect"? Then, you find out that this is not what you actually need. Maybe your actions have resulted in a delay in treatment which would have effectively controlled your condition, given an earlier start date. Maybe you start experiencing problematic side-effects and stop the drug for that reason. Then, what do you get for your efforts? Your bad LDL cholesterol levels may increase, but not to the level set by the health insurance company. Maybe you're just borderline or high risk, and not critical. You don't meet the level specified by the health insurance company, and the request is denied. Seems like a no-win scenario for the patient.

Wait a minute. How about the health insurance company helping you prevent a full-blown situation <u>before</u> it happens (primary prevention), rather than waiting for problems to happen and then treating the condition (secondary prevention)? For example, your tracking process starts with your bad LDL cholesterol levels falling within the borderline range. As time goes on, your levels steadily increase until they get into the beginning of the "high" range, and remain there. Remember, people with chronic kidney disease are already at a higher risk of developing (or may already have) cardiovascular disease. Bad (LDL) cholesterol is one of the substances which, if allowed to form plaque by building-up in the arteries, can develop into atherosclerosis (narrowing and hardening of the arteries). Cholesterol plaque can block arteries in the kidneys, resulting in functions shutting down.

Being in this "high, but not quite high enough" range is problematic and possibly life-threatening, given the medical condition. However, it is still not high enough to satisfy the health insurance company. Personally, I find it to be inconceivable that a financial institution that sells insurance has the right to determine for a human being what level of bad LDL cholesterol qualifies as "high enough," let alone how long a life must be jeopardized by allowing that level to persist.

For every action, there is a consequence. It's a given that you will pay a price; but, you may not know how high it will be until it comes due.

CHAPTER 16:
My Body, My Choice

<u>Reason for denial</u>: <u>The specialty area of the doctor/practitioner requesting the medication was not deemed appropriate by the health insurance company. The health insurance company would not approve coverage.</u>

The people of the fantasy city of Caring were lucky. They never had to deal with *the Chaos Cohorts*. They would never suspect there was any force strong enough to entice some doctors/practitioners to turn away from the ethical and moral values which were the foundation of their profession and which they took an oath to uphold.

The story is quite different for those of us who live in the real world. In the United States, branches of *the Chaos Cohorts* have been allowed to create and enforce rules that do nothing less than undermine the authority of ethical and compassionate doctors/practitioners. It is unfortunate, but true, that *the Chaos Cohorts* will attempt to take everything away from patients, to include their dignity and freedom to make their own decisions. They expect you to follow them without question. Controlling entities often have double standards. *The Chaos Cohorts* fall into this category. They want to make all of the rules and don't want to be challenged about any of the rules that they make.

These entities seem to want to control the very choices that patients make, especially those having to do with who will represent them. Luckily there are other power players out there who understand what this *Alliance* is trying to do, and have taken steps in an attempt to counter them. When it comes to representation, patients do have the right to choose their own agents.

Every doctor's/practitioner's office that I have ever been in has a copy of what's known as the *Patient's Bill of Rights* (otherwise known as *HIPPA*) posted in a prominent position. A copy of this *Bill of Rights* is usually included in the paperwork given to a patient, and requires a signature documenting that you have reviewed and understand the contents. This *Bill of Rights* was created to make sure that patient needs were being met fairly, to emphasize the benefit of good patient – health care provider relationships, and to make sure that everyone understood rights and responsibilities involved in supporting good health.

This *Bill of Rights* gives patients the authority to take part in their own treatment decisions, and to know their own treatment options. Patients have a right to choose someone who will represent them as agents in all matters related to health care, to include family members, guardians or others.

As a caregiver, how many times have staff members at doctor's/practitioner's offices or at hospitals asked whether or not you have a "Health Care Power of Attorney" document? They usually won't share any information concerning a patient unless you can produce a copy of this document showing that you are their appointed representative.

Giving someone else authority to make decisions on your behalf in what could easily be life-and-death matters, is not to be taken lightly. The choice of this representative should be deliberate and well considered. What better choice for this position is there than your own doctor/practitioner, especially when it comes to decisions about prescription medication? Who is better qualified to act in this capacity than this person, especially when it comes to requesting appropriate life-saving medication on your behalf?

The best of all worlds would be that your doctor/practitioner is also your friend. Now, I know that some people will argue that this might represent a conflict of interest. Maybe there are drugs that this doctor/practitioner personally favors or gets incentives to promote. Maybe this doctor/practitioner has an ownership interest in the biopharmaceutical company that makes the medication. Appointing anyone to this position implies that you have thoroughly vetted this person regarding status and their willingness to carry out your wishes. It is also understood that there is a bond of trust between the two of you, and that you have confidence in their absolute willingness and capacity to uphold their promise to you. Personally, I would rather give this duty to a person with whom I already have a positive, on-going, working relationship. This foundation and understanding should be enough to eliminate any possibility of personal interests getting in the way of their responsibility to act as your agent and to make decisions for your whole well-being.

Note that the health insurance company doesn't say that you can't appoint a doctor/practitioner as your agent. They just want the power to tell you which doctor/practitioner you can appoint (see Appendix T, Letter dated August 15, 2017).

Let's say that, knowing your rights under the *Bill of Rights*, you proceed to make your own choice. The doctor/practitioner of your choice plays a principal role in your case, but does not practice in one of the specialty areas designated by the health insurance company. You might argue that your choice is the one and only doctor/practitioner who always takes the leadership role in coordinating your overall treatment plan (and making sure that it gets implemented), because the other "specialists" either "don't have, or don't want to, or won't take" the time to communicate with each other. You might argue that the other "specialists" are not familiar with the over-all picture of your needs given your medical condition and are recommending a remedy that is not in your best interest. You might argue that you don't need the additional stress of having to establish a new relationship with a new medical professional.

How many times have you experienced the "thrill" of calling for a "new patient" doctor/practitioner appointment and being put on a waiting list, sometimes for weeks? If there is an emergency, and you call after hours, a pre-recorded message will instruct you to go directly to the hospital emergency room. Heaven forbid that you are new to two or more "specialists," with differing opinions about the necessity of a medication. Your need as a patient could get lost in a battle of physician egos, with you ultimately being the one to lose the war.

When there is a longstanding relationship of trust and respect between a patient and his/her doctor/practitioner, then it's only natural for that patient to delegate the responsibility of medical representative and advocate on his/her behalf to that doctor/practitioner. You might make that decision on the basis of both tangible (for example, professional certifications or track record) and intangible (for example, kindness or integrity) factors. The important thing is that you make the decision, because it is your right to do so. You choose a doctor/practitioner as your representative, because you have some kind of a positive connection. You understand and respect each other.

The bottom line for the health insurance company seems to be how much "money" they can get from you, as well as how far you will allow them to control what they do to you without complaint. That is the extent of their relationship with you. It is impersonal. What is the sense of letting someone, with whom you have no personal connection, tell you who you can designate to make life or death decisions when it comes to your health and welfare?

CHAPTER 17
The In-Crowd

<u>Reason for denial: The patient was not diagnosed with one of the specific forms of bad cholesterol sanctioned by the insurance company. The insurance company would not approve coverage.</u>

Another way for a patient to get approval for a pharmaceutical drug through the prior authorization process is to qualify due to a diagnosis of one of the conditions authorized by the health insurance company (a financial institution that sells insurance and one branch of *the Chaos Cohorts*). Consider, for example, how this might work for a patient like Walt who is already diagnosed with kidney disease, has too much bad LDL cholesterol in his blood, can't take statin drugs, and can only tolerate one non-statin prescription medication.

As mentioned in chapter nine, Familial Hypercholesterolaemia (FH) is a genetic disorder which may result from having too much bad LDL cholesterol in your blood. There are two forms of FH: <u>Heterozygous Familial Hypercholesterolemia</u> (HeFH), which is inherited when only one of your parents has it; and, <u>Homozygous Familial Hypercholesterolemia (HoFH)</u>, which is inherited when both of your parents have it. A diagnosis of either one of these conditions would qualify Walt for the non-statin prescription medication that he needs. Walt does not have either one of these conditions. That's a big negative for him, as far as the health insurance company is concerned.

Another condition sanctioned by Walt's health insurance company which would automatically qualify him for the non-statin medication he needs to control his bad LDL cholesterol is "Clinical Atherosclerotic Cardiovascular Disease" (ASCVD). As mentioned in chapter nine, if bad LDL cholesterol is allowed to build-up in the arteries, it can form plaque which can lead to atherosclerosis (narrowing and hardening of the arteries). This build-up can cause a heart attack or a stroke. Just imagine what having a condition like this means for a patient with kidney disease and on dialysis. This is why it's crucial that Walt's bad LDL cholesterol be controlled, because he already has a diagnosis of hypertension.

There is no doubt that, given his symptoms, Walt meets the criteria for a diagnosis of ASCVD (Atherosclerotic Cardiovascular Disease). There is one catch. No matter how many of his other doctors/practitioners are willing to put their professional careers on the line by certifying, in writing, that he has ASCVD, a diagnosis made by a cardiologist is the only diagnosis that the health insurance company will accept (see Appendices O and R, First and Second Letters of Medical Necessity; and Appendix P, Letter dated March 8, 2017). The prior authorization process stops if this diagnostician is not involved and willing to do this.

There are many ways that a cardiologist could delay or end the process for Walt, especially one who might be less than favorable about participating in the process to begin with. Our experience has been that sometimes it's almost like the cardiologists are working for the health insurance company and not for him.

Walt is no different than any other patient. He wants his doctor/practitioner to have the best training and experience possible, especially in his/her specialty area. In addition to excellent professional credentials, finding a cardiologist who has a friendly and positive bedside manner would definitely make for a "good day."

Honestly, I don't know about cardiologists. The ones that we have encountered act like they don't want to be bothered, especially when you question what they tell you to do. Now, I'm not referring to all cardiologists, just the ones we have come in contact with. I'm sure that there must be some supportive ones out there, somewhere. Our experience with the cardiologists involved with Walt's case serve as examples. Walt initially had a cardiologist who seemed to be a pretty nice guy, until we questioned him about a drug that he wanted to prescribe for another condition that Walt has. Doctors/Practitioners who prescribed this other drug were known to end up in litigation due to the adverse side effects (for example, it could kill you). Consistent with my responsibility as my husband's caregiver, I pointed this out to this cardiologist (in a nice way, of course). The cardiologist threw a very loud temper tantrum, accused me of not having Walt's best interest at heart, and said that we questioned his judgment. This tantrum was so loud that people in the outer hallway knocked on the door to see what was happening. Needless to say, that cardiologist went "bye-bye."

The next cardiologist was congenial, as long as he could stare into his computer for almost the entire length of the office visit, and was not questioned about his recommendations. His attachment to his computer during office visits became so pronounced that I starting calling him "computer man." Of course, this was only behind his back. That relationship didn't last long. In fact, we left his practice to go to a third cardiologist.

Walt was referred to a third cardiologist through the Veterans Administration (VA). We sent all of the paperwork that we had collected about Walt's case to this cardiologist about two weeks prior to the initial office visit. We wanted to give him a "heads-up," because we knew about the standard fifteen- to- twenty minute per visit rule. This information included data from the doctor/practitioner (nephrologist) who initiated the prior authorization process, stating that the pharmaceutical drug was a "medical necessity" needed to control Walt's bad LDL cholesterol (see Appendices O and R). It was noted, in bold print, that Walt could not take statin medications. We also included the results of a preventive health screening (which we paid for out-of-pocket) which confirmed the presence of Atherosclerotic Cardiovascular Disease (ASCVD). There was enough information to support a diagnosis of ASCVD, which would have satisfied one of the prerequisites mandated by the health insurance company.

We believed that we were all on the same page and that this cardiologist was going to advocate on Walt's behalf. He verbally admitted that the drug recommended by Walt's nephrologist would more than do the job controlling his bad LDL cholesterol, and even gave Walt "free" samples of this drug that he had in his office. He just happened to have them, because he already had a few patients in his practice on this particular medication. His staff also gave Walt more free samples during subsequent visits.

Everything was great, at least for a while. We were absolutely shocked by the events that followed. This same cardiologist, when formally contacted by the health insurance company to provide written information needed for prior authorization, "reconsidered" his position. What happened next involved him making so many twists and turns that it would have put the best contortionist to shame.

This cardiologist told Walt (by way of one of his nurses) that he needed to make another appointment for an office visit so that the "situation" could be discussed. What situation? The only appointment opening was almost one month beyond the time limit deadline set by the health insurance company for return of the requested information.

From that point on, it seemed like this cardiologist was working for the health insurance company and not for Walt. This cardiologist said that he wanted Walt to go through a *STEP* process, which basically amounted to an evaluation of the effects of a series of less expensive and weaker statin medications in order to prove that they didn't work before going on the drug which would work, but was more expensive. When we reminded him that Walt could not take statins, this cardiologist said that there was nothing more that he could do for him. He acknowledged that his decision would condemn Walt to suffer the adverse consequences of a build-up of bad LDL cholesterol.

Questions from us as to why he was going back on his promise to advocate for the appropriate pharmaceutical medication resulted in this cardiologist labeling Walt as a "difficult" patient. Heaven only knows what label I was given! He dropped Walt from his caseload and told him to come to his office and pick-up his file. This cardiologist said that he had talked with Walt's nephrologist, who told him that he did not qualify for the drug. (Representatives from the nephrologist's office said that this did not happen.) He said that he had made several attempts to obtain "case notes" from the nephrologist, with no success. (Representatives from the nephrologist's office said that the cardiologist never sent a required "release of information" form to them so that the notes could be provided.) He then tried to "pass the buck," telling Walt that he needed to go back to the "second" cardiologist (computer man) who had not seen Walt for some time. His rationale was that the second cardiologist had "history" with Walt. My best guess is that he didn't like being questioned, had second thoughts about everything he would have to send to the health insurance company, and didn't want to interact with someone who was not willing to play a subservient role. The bottom line was that we knew too much and asked too many questions. The name, address and telephone number of this cardiologist would probably be found in the telephone directory of the fantasy city of Chaos.

At this point, Walt has yet to find a cardiologist with enough professional integrity to advocate for him so that he can get the appropriate prescription medication he needs. This third cardiologist admitted that Walt needed to control his bad LDL cholesterol, and that taking the pharmaceutical drug in question would more than do the job. He was more than willing to provide a few free samples "under the table." However, he refused to give formal written approval in support of the drug unless Walt took additional steps. Taking those steps would most likely be dangerous for Walt. What caused this cardiologist to go back on his word? Why on earth would he be hesitant to legitimize in writing what he apparently knew in his heart was the right course of action?

In order to be beyond reproach (at lease in his mind), and legitimize a right to the appropriate medication, this cardiologist "highly" recommended that Walt either: (1) undergo a potentially life-threatening procedure called an angiogram; or, (2) get into a clinical trial group. That way, Walt could get the diagnostic label needed to satisfy the health insurance company, prior authorization approval, and a legitimate prescription. However, this authorization would come from someone else, thereby relieving this cardiologist from any ownership of assigning a diagnostic label. I wonder if he would take a stand for any patient other than one who was so sick that he/she was almost dead.

None of these options are realistic for Walt. Given his chronological age and other medical conditions, Walt might not survive an angiogram. As there are no clinical trial groups going on in our city, locating one and traveling what might be a great distance, would most certainly present problems. This would interfere with Walt's dialysis schedule and compromise his already fragile health. As was true for participants in the Tuskegee Study, there is no guarantee that Walt would get anything other than a placebo as a clinical trial group participant. He does not have that kind of time to waste.

Walt is between cardiologists at this time. This is not good, because he has a diagnosis of hypertension. His doctor/physician (nephrologist) is trying to find someone for him, hopefully who is knowledgeable about issues related to kidney disease and hemodialysis. We have found no cardiologist to date who will make this critical diagnosis in writing of ASCVD, which the health insurance company says that he does not have (see Appendix Q, Letter dated June 7, 2017). They refuse to officially document in writing that the drug is necessary to control Walt's bad LDL cholesterol. They demand additional health outcomes data, to justify him getting something that we already know works for him.

Agents of the health insurance company branch of *the Chaos Cohorts* want to dictate a course of action, without considering (or caring about) consequences for Walt. Apparently this doctor/practitioner carries out their orders, or fears them enough, to disregard the patient's needs. Once again, the resolution of this dilemma will take time that Walt may or may not have, and involves making choices which may not be entirely in his best interest.

CHAPTER 18
Health Outcomes Data and Clinical Trials

Why would a cardiologist recommend that Walt enroll in a clinical trial group to legitimize his right to what is already an appropriate pharmaceutical drug? What would be the value of this being used as a way of getting the diagnostic label needed to satisfy the health insurance company, prior authorization, and a legitimate prescription?

First of all, it's important to know what data is. Generally speaking, data is information. Information is usually collected for a purpose, such as to do something with it. People are curious by nature. Data collection and analysis can be thought of as tools used to satisfy this curiosity. How much and what kind of data is collected depends upon the purpose it will be used for.

Sometimes data is collected from a large number of people, so that predictions can be made about how something will influence individuals or smaller groups. Most people know about this kind of purpose. Research that is conducted in order to learn what will happen, for example, if a health care intervention takes place is called outcomes research. The goal is to ultimately improve the quality of care received.

Biopharmaceutical companies (one branch of *the Chaos Cohorts*) do this all the time, mainly to help with sales. Remarks about some positive finding revealed during the research process are common features of marketing campaigns.

Another reason that they do this is to discover how well a new prescription medication works. They might target patients having defined characteristics, then collect lab test results (for example, lipid test results) to see if a specific treatment caused a change in the patients' health.

Health outcome data are products of clinical trials. A clinical trial is an experiment/test or observation that is run by investigator(s) (for example, medical doctors/practitioners). When drugs are involved, the trial is designed to test how the drugs affect people. Participants get specific interventions (for example, medications) during a series of phases (defined by the Food and Drug Administration, FDA), as determined by a protocol or research plan. The drug manufacturer (for example, a biopharmaceutical company) develops the protocol (instructional manual).

Making a decision to participate in a clinical trial should be taken very seriously. Clinical trials have their positive features. They have also been criticized for a number of reasons. One reason is that participants may not be told whether they are getting a new drug or just a sugar pill (placebo) that contains no active ingredients.

Another criticism is that researchers may not tell participants the whole truth about different aspects of the study. Once concluded, researchers have been known to highlight the positive study outcomes and to leave out what went wrong. Advertisements by means of television commercials are notorious for doing this. Most of the air- time advertising a drug includes eye-catching graphics, wonderful animation, and plenty of award-winning dialogue praising positive features. The final five or six seconds (if that long) involves a string of possible side effects and precautions, delivered at a low volume, by a fast-talking voice-over talent, who barely takes a breath of air until finished.

Researchers may communicate differently with participants when describing placebos and specific procedures. While it is standard operating procedure to discuss the main elements of a study with participants (for example, objectives, voluntary or paid participation), and answer questions (informed consent), this difference in communication could be thought of as deception. For example, researchers may give a drug to participants in one group who have high levels of bad LDL cholesterol to see whether their levels decrease. They may not in another group. Participants might not be informed as to what they are getting.

Participants can be harmed during clinical trials. However, the risk of being harmed during a clinical trial might be equivalent to those that would be expected during the typical course of any illness.

Protocols (instructional manuals) contain rules for choosing participants for trial groups. They may have specific health conditions that the researchers want to study. An example of this is when the only participants allowed to participate are those who are healthy with no pre-existing medical conditions.

CHAPTER 19
Trial Group Participation – The FDA

Most consumers are aware of the role played by the Food and Drug Administration (FDA) when products need to be recalled due to defects or the potential to cause harm. The public is alerted and recalls are started. Did you know that the FDA is a government regulatory agency within the U.S. Department of Health and Human Services? This agency can't regulate the cost of drugs, but it does give approval so that they can be sold. As is true for most agencies, funding is needed to offset expenditures and budgets need to be created. It would be interesting to find out how the FDA budget is funded and where the majority of that funding comes from (hint – from pharmaceutical companies).[5]

The FDA is organized into six centers; however, the center which oversees prescription and over-the-counter drugs is the *Center for Drug Evaluation and Research* (CDER).[6] Drug companies send their applications to this center for review and approval. Clinical trials (for example, in humans) must be reviewed by the FDA before they can start.

The FDA then provides a series of instructions, as determined by the research instruction manual (protocol). An example of this might be instructions regarding the "phase" during which patients get interventions (for example, medications).

The following demonstrates the sequence of steps and stages that a biopharmaceutical company would take when requesting approval from the FDA to market a new drug.[7]

The first step, called "preclinical testing," takes an average of three to four years, and involves using the drug on animals and in laboratory studies to note effectiveness and safety issues.

The second step requires the biopharmaceutical company to file an Investigational New Drug Application (IND), and marks the beginning of testing the drug on people. This application includes information such as: the results of prior experiments and a listing of any harmful effects found during the animal studies. This information is then reviewed by the Institutional Review Board (IRB). Approval from this Board marks the start of the Clinical Trial Phase study, which can take an average of six to seven years.

CHAPTER 20:
You've Got to Get What You Need

A buildup of bad LDL cholesterol can form plaque, which can then develop into atherosclerosis or coronary artery disease (for example, heart attack or stroke). People with chronic kidney disease are at a higher risk of developing (or may already have) cardiovascular disease. This is certainly true in Walt's case. He is not alone, as there are many patients diagnosed with this condition.

Why are there so many people with this condition, given the fact that there is a lipid lowering medication already on the market which could more than adequately remedy the situation? What is keeping this medication from the masses needing access to it?

One answer might be that in order to be considered, your characteristics must match the characteristics of clinical trial group participants. Otherwise, an argument can be made that the same results might not be true for you, and prior authorization will be denied. This control is regulated by criteria sanctioned by two branches of *the Chaos Cohorts*, the health insurance company and the biopharmaceutical company. Additional back-up comes from the pharmacy benefit management company (PBM).

New criteria upon which to make decisions regarding access will not be forthcoming unless additional trials are conducted, which include broader participant characteristics. This could go on and on. The question becomes, "how much is enough?"

Then, there are doctors/practitioners who, for whatever reason, seem to be fearful of going against what the health insurance company and biopharmaceutical company mandate. This becomes a problem when those medical professionals are the only ones recognized as able to give input to the decision making process, such as cardiologists. There are those who put-off making timely decisions, using the excuse that they need to get more and more data. This leaves a lot of patients who could benefit from targeted drug right now literally out in the cold.

Let's face it. There are some cardiologists who just don't know how to work the system in order to help their patients qualify for the prescription medication in question. Conversations with caregivers who have found cardiologists able to overcome barriers to prior authorization reveal that these doctors/practitioners have one thing in common. They hire the "right" staff people to get the job done. Sometimes they will train existing staff members in what to do. They basically have one duty, and that is learning how to work the prior authorization process so that requests get approved. They know what is required, and how requests should be written. That's how they get the job done.

In Walt's case, the health insurance company was unwilling to approve his prior authorization request. He could not find a cardiologist willing to do the right thing, let alone one who had the "right" people on staff. None of them were willing to put into writing that Walt has ASCVD, which would have qualified him for the medication (see Appendices P and Q). Also, some of his characteristics differed from those of the clinical trial participants used in the study and upon which the criteria was established. That study protocol included specific participant characteristics (for example, Familial Hypercholesterolaemia status).

The health insurance company rubber-stamped the protocol established by the biopharmaceutical company, which closed off access to the prescription medication for anyone who needed it but did not have the same characteristics. Those characteristics were chosen by the biopharmaceutical company and the health insurance company (branches of *the Chaos Cohorts*), and only included a few studies which looked at participants having a common, genetic form of high (bad) LDL cholesterol who might benefit from lipid-lowering medications. While he has ASCVD, Walt does not have these genetic conditions. The fact that the medication was right for them did not justify withholding it from others in need. Keeping this drug away from others on this basis was in effect, discrimination.

Additional trials might produce findings making it possible for many, many more people to benefit from the drug, rather than just a select group. While this might happen in the future, Walt needs access right now.

Things were not helped by the fact that Walt was unable to find a cardiologist who was willing to "think outside of the box" and certify (in writing) the presence of a condition which was obvious to his other doctors/practitioners. Unfortunately, these branches of *the Chaos Cohorts* were not interested or concerned with what his other doctors/practitioner's (especially his nephrologist) had to say. They also had no concern that the truth be told. I guess that these cardiologists are still waiting for more data.

I mentioned during the dedication of this book that when all else fails, "keep it light, because the dark side is just too heavy." If push comes to shove, Walt could go on indefinitely getting free samples of this drug. However, it would be much better if he qualified for a legitimate prescription, because the inconsistency factor would be removed from the equation. I have also heard (via the grapevine) that the day will soon come when drug company sales representatives start limiting the number of free samples currently given-out. It seems that some doctors/practitioners are giving them to patients who need this medication but can't get prior authorization approval. Imagine that!

Walt has multiple medical issues. A legitimate prescription for the medication which controls his bad LDL cholesterol levels will make this one less thing to worry about. He needs to get this drug on a regular basis and as soon as possible

CHAPTER 21
Misuse and Abuse

Health insurance plans can be purchased in many ways, such as privately or by enrolling in one provided through the government. Health insurance companies have often been recognized for their role in providing safeguards against unreasonable rate increases. There is no argument that the goal of protecting consumers is a good reason for them to exist, and positive things do happen. Health Maintenance Organizations (HMO's) are examples of state regulated health insurance plans, and there are some good ones out there.

While they serve a purpose, health insurance companies have been criticized on a number of points such as charging too much money for coverage, small claim settlements, and sizeable executive salaries.

Despite all of their positive accomplishments, a health insurance company is still one of the four branches of *the Chaos Cohorts*. When it comes to the prior authorization process, the biopharmaceutical company gives input, but the health insurance company is the only entity with the power to say what qualifies as being a medical necessity. Patients have no input into this process.

Health insurance companies will not pay for pharmaceutical drugs requiring medical prescriptions which they don't authorize, even though your doctor/practitioner prescribes the medication and labels it as a medical necessity. These companies may or may not get back to the doctor/practitioner to let him/her know that they denied approval. They want to maintain control of access to the drug, and thereby mandate that it will be given only to those meeting specific diagnostic criteria (of their choosing, and with the biopharmaceutical company's blessing), with no consideration as to how it might benefit others who also need it to control their bad LDL cholesterol. In Walt's case, he has a level of bad LDL cholesterol that needs to be reduced, period. That reduction needs to take place as quickly as possible, because he is diagnosed with hypertension, is 87 years old, has kidney disease, and is on dialysis. Taking the drug requested by his doctor/practitioner (nephrologist) is the only way that this reduction will happen.

An appeal process can always be initiated in the event that the prior authorization request is denied. However, the appeal must go through the health insurance company's own internal review process. This is like the fox guarding the hen house.

Because the health insurance company holds the power to determine whether or not an authorization request is approved or denied, the decisions they make could easily determine whether a patient lives or dies. This is where the potential for abuse and misuse comes in. The company might, for example, deny authorization, and instead require that a patient first pursue a course of action which demonstrates that other medications are not successful in treating the medical condition. Of course, these other medications may be those favored by the health insurance company or of a lesser cost. There is obviously no concern for how this might make a patient feel or other issues which might be created. The patient is the only one concerned about being caused unnecessary pain, suffering, and lost time.

This raises a number of questions. What gives someone who has never met you, or knows nothing about the particulars of your medical situation, the power to make life and death decisions about you and your health care? What gives them the right to question a request made by your doctor/practitioner of record? What credentials qualify these people for this purpose? Regardless of the answers to these questions, know that your doctor/practitioner had nothing to do with this process. It was your health insurance company.

CHAPTER 22:
Just Below the Surface

A universal truth is that all things have a starting point. In the case of prescription medications, all things start with the branch of *the Chaos Cohorts* known as the biopharmaceutical company. They are the ones who actually make the drugs.

The process starts with a drug company picking a medical problem that it thinks it might be able to do something about. Then the company tests many drugs over a specified time period to find the one that is most likely to correct the identified medical problem. In the process, criteria are determined as to who is eligible to receive the drug and who is not eligible, which as mentioned earlier, smacks of discrimination.

Criteria, in and of itself, is not a bad thing, because it sets a standard by which something can be measured. The problem arises when a drug is advertised and marketed to the general public without making it clear that there will be some who might not qualify for it, along with what it takes to qualify for it. Otherwise, misunderstandings happen. Hope is given to those who in reality, won't qualify for it to begin with. How cruel is this?

Once the biopharmaceutical company identifies a medical problem and conducts testing, their information is sent to the FDA for approval so that the drug can be sold on the market. Being able to sell the drug and make money is the goal of the biopharmaceutical company.

When FDA approval is given, the way is clear for the drug to be sold on the market, either through a mail home delivery service, or patient pick-up at the community, neighborhood pharmacy. If there is any doubt about the legitimacy of a request, a pharmacist can refuse to fill a prescription. [8] One example of this might be when prior authorization is needed, but there is no record of it being received. The pharmacist is a health care provider and not to blame for this action. He/she is just following orders. Not following the process could result in charges of malpractice, fines and/or loss of license to practice.

There is no argument that biopharmaceutical companies make medications which can help people. However, there are a number of ways that these companies can cause problems for patients and doctors/practitioners. One example involves how they market and advertise pharmaceutical drugs. Biopharmaceutical companies hire sales representatives. These sales representatives go to doctors/practitioner's offices to introduce the drugs that they want them to use. Sales representatives are usually working for "pharmacy benefit management companies (PBM's)", or a "wholesaler" who has gotten the drug from the biopharmaceutical company. How many times have you had to wait to see your own doctor/practitioner until the drug company sales representative has finished making a sales pitch? It has been my experience that they just go to the check-in window and present a business card – all on a walk-in basis. Never mind it that you had a set appointment time, maybe booked weeks in advance.

In Walt's case, there is only one pharmaceutical drug that will lower his bad LDL cholesterol, because he can't take statin drugs. It is a medication which is given by injection. So far he has been able to get free samples. These free samples are supplied by the sales representatives who visit his doctors/practitioners. So, in some ways, the interaction between the sales representatives and his doctors/practitioners works in his favor. The down-side is that he does not get the samples unless the sales representative brings them to the doctors/practitioner's office, which can really impact when he is able to take what he needs.

Walt's doctors/practitioners told him about the pharmaceutical drug needed to control his bad LDL cholesterol. He did not approach his doctors/practitioners for it. His case serves as a good example of how advertising and marketing strategies used by the biopharmaceutical company impact patient care.

A major way that this particular drug is advertised to the public is through television commercials. Some of the information is accurate. Other critical information is either misleading or missing.

The way in which the drug is advertised gives the impression that it's available to anyone in need, is "heaven sent," and can work miracles. The truth is that it really does what it is advertised to do.

My concern is that factors are not mentioned which disqualify a patient from getting the medication, such as not having a referring doctor/practitioner who practices within a specific specialty area accepted by the health insurance company, or that approval is based upon a patient having a specified genetic disorder or diagnostic label. They build you up and then let you down.

Walt's doctors/practitioners know that he needs this pharmaceutical drug, so they are willing to help him stay alive by giving him free samples, pending a decision about prior authorization. The cardiologists, for whatever reason, are the ones keeping the process from moving forward. Both Walt and I pray that there will be a light for him at the end of the tunnel.

CHAPTER 23
A Rose by Any Other Name

What comes to mind when I mention the word, discrimination? Do you consider making judgments as discrimination, like having a preference for the color red versus green, or having a desire for a cheeseburger rather than a pizza? The fact is that people discriminate in favor of one thing or another. There is nothing wrong with this, except when those judgments have the backing of laws and regulations which put individuals (or groups) at a disadvantage. If all other factors are equal, consider what happens when an individual (or a group) is given preferential treatment because of specified characteristic, like racial heritage.

Discriminatory practices become detrimental when used as strategies meant to do harm to people. There is a problem when such practices result in unfair treatment which grants favors to one person (or to a group) and excludes others. Let's relate this to health care. What if patients having certain characteristics are seen as being more entitled to access certain life-saving pharmaceutical drugs requiring medical prescriptions, when compared to patients who don't have those characteristics? What if those characteristics are specified as the only qualifying criteria for that drug? What about patient's who don't have those characteristics, but still need that drug? What are they supposed to do? Both groups need access; and, this is the only remedy that will work. Criteria, in and of itself, is not a bad thing, because it sets a standard by which something can be measured. The problem arises when a drug is advertised and marketed to the general public without making it clear that there will be some who might qualify for it, some who might not qualify for it, and what is needed to qualify for it. This is how the prescription medication that Walt needs is being advertised.

I can understand why some biopharmaceutical manufacturers would not want to make this clear up-front. It might be difficult to come up with reasons supporting their decision to discriminate, intentionally or unintentionally, especially in cases calling for life-saving medication. There are no words to describe someone who would take away what could possibly be a person's only hope for life, let alone for a better quality of life. Personally, I could not imagine how it would feel to admit that I played a role in deciding who would get a life-saving pharmaceutical drug and who would be denied access. Caring about the welfare of others is one of the things that I like about myself. I can't speak for anyone else.

CHAPTER 24:
It Starts at the Top

It's October 2017. Today is just another day as my husband's caregiver. I have high expectations that all will go well and that the day will be relatively stress free. That would be nice for a change.

I like to start each day by turning on the television and listening to local and national news events such as national security issues, sports and weather reports. Today, the health care system is in the spotlight. This time it's big news!

As the caregiver of a kidney dialysis patient, any news having to do with healthcare in this country grabs my attention. As the caregiver of a veteran of mixed race, who is on hemodialysis, any news like this puts me on high alert!

Plans have been put into motion which will start the process of ending the *Patient Protection and Affordable Care Act*. The particulars of what such a change will entail are not clear at this time, which should be of great concern to every citizen and especially to caregivers of patients in need of pharmaceutical drugs requiring medical prescriptions.

As the caregiver of a kidney dialysis patient, my life is already full of uncertainties – how long will my husband live on dialysis, what can he eat; and how to manage pain, diarrhea, constipation, nausea, anemia and motivational issues. I don't appreciate having anything else added to my "worry" list, which is already overflowing with possibilities.

Who is responsible for this chaos and confusion? Given the magnitude of this action, there can be only one answer. The President of the United States, using the powers of the executive branch of the government, is on a mission to restructure our health care system by putting "something" in place. What he wants to put into place seems to change, almost on a daily basis. The resulting chaos and confusion created by this uncertainty are well-known tactics, and the hallmark of *the Chaos Cohorts*. Be afraid! Be very afraid!

Our government, the executive branch of *the Chaos Cohorts*, continues to use the same old tactics (lies, deception, apathy), that were employed to deceive so many people back in 1948. The only difference is that they have become more sophisticated and out in the open with the passing of time. These diversions occupy so much of our attention that we have little energy left for identifying and addressing what really matters. Efforts which were once directed primarily at defined groups in this country are now being extended to every citizen, from sea-to-shining sea.

There is no doubt that as caregivers, we already have more than enough on our to-do lists and don't need extra issues to worry about. A closer look would probably reveal some things that could be eliminated, because they are not priorities. One thing that we must keep up with is what's happening in the political arena. What's going on right now with the proposed changes that our President wants to make is the very reason why we should make time each day to monitor this. The fate of those we care for is being determined by deals made between the federal government, health insurance companies, distributors (pharmacy benefit management companies and wholesale drug distributors), and biopharmaceutical companies.

The unilateral action taken by our President in the form of an executive order to start the restructuring of America's health care system, along with all of the confusion and controversy around it, is an excellent example of the brains of *the Chaos Cohorts* at work. As of this date, I don't think that there is anyone in this country who can say with absolute certainty, that he/she knows what we have in place to deal with the healthcare needs of our citizens. Something is happening in the form of a change; but, whatever that is seems to take different forms, almost on a daily basis. The one constant factor is what the President will do in the event that he finds fault with what is given to him. If past behavior is a predictor of future behavior, then he will literally throw it out of the window. Everything starts over again.

The following two events illustrate how the executive branch of our government (the brains of *the Chaos Cohorts*) uses the tactics of lies, deception, apathy and confusion to create distractions.

The first event happened a few weeks ago when the President signed an executive order to start restructuring America's health care system. He suspended this executive order, and turned the matter over to others to work-out the details. They gave him what they worked on; however, he didn't like the product which came from a bipartisan effort. Therefore, nothing could go to Congress for a vote to determine whether the *Patient Protection and Affordable Care Act* could be repealed. Then someone posed a question about possibly "band-aiding" what we already had in place, which would keep it on the books for the for-seeable future.

At this point, it's still around (minus financial penalties for people who do not carry health insurance). Oh, my aching head!

December 2, 2017 marked the date of the second event. On that date, the Senate approved a (Republican) Tax Bill by a vote of 51 to 49. The process used in getting this to a vote was criticized by those who opposed it (basically Democrats). Criticisms included: (1) the speed of the Tax Bill; (2) the last-minute changes that were made; and, (3) having little time to review those changes. One senator, a Democrat, was shown on television holding up a page of the Tax Bill which included "handwritten notes" – changes which were scribbled in the margins. What was handwritten appeared illegible, resulting in this senator recommending that caution be used before taking further actions. So much for reading the small print, even if given the opportunity.

Whatever happens, there are two things that we can count on. First, there is no question that all citizens should be concerned about the actions taking place, because some kind of fundamental change is in the making. Second, there is no doubt that we are going to have to pay some amount of money in order to get some level of health care in this country. Sadly for some veterans, this means that the promise of free health care which was made so long ago will still go unrealized.

I predict that history will refer to the signing (and eventual passing by Congress) of a new executive health care order as being one of the defining moments of this century. Unfortunately, many are taking advantage of the current political climate as an opportunity to show the world the worst that our country has to offer. With all of the deception and bickering that's going on, it's difficult to distinguish the lies from the half-truths. The "light of all lights" is shining brightly, both in the fantasy city of Chaos and in the United States.

CHAPTER 25
The Devil is in the Details

I can remember a time when it was almost a sin not to watch daytime soap operas. The weekly episodes seemed to be filled with mystery, melodrama and juicy topics. My mother and grandmother were faithful followers. I would venture to guess that today something else vies for the attention of the soap-opera audience. That "something else" is network news.

I have never been a particular fan of network news shows. Now it seems that this is the first thing that I watch in the morning and the last thing that I watch before going to bed. There is plenty of commentary about how people are suffering or being exploited in one way or another, what's happening on the world scene, and what the United States government is up to.

Unfortunately, I have found that most of the stories are negative, especially where our government is concerned. The use of tactics such as lies, deception, confusion and apathy by government officials appears to provide more than enough material for comedians on late night television shows.

Remember my mentioning that the devil is in the details? Back in 1948, many tactics were used by our government to entice young men of mixed race heritage to voluntarily enlist, or at least not to resist being drafted into service.

The government was pretty good at doing this. For African American soldiers on active duty, the promotion of a false sense of security redirected their attention away from the atrocities which were really being committed in the civilian arena. African American soldiers, upon returning to civilian life, found that racism, segregation and discrimination were continuing as usual. Many found it hard to reconcile this reality, let alone to trust in the powers that be.

Getting the votes of African Americans made it possible for President Truman to win the 1948 election. However, many questioned his true motives and commitment as far as improving the plight of African Americans in this country. Was he really concerned or just giving lip service to accomplish a self-serving goal? With the passing of time, the realization of being lied to and betrayed by this government has gradually come into clear focus, but only after attempts at redirection and deception were recognized.

Well, guess what? While it is true that signs restricting the use of public restrooms and restaurants based on race have been removed, the spirit of racism, and the insensitivity which often accompanies it, is still alive and well in the United States. *The Chaos Cohorts* are well aware of what appears to be an apparent growing racial separation in this country, and use the confusion and drama associated with it to direct attention away from what they are doing.

The product of this redirection may last for a few hours or days. I compare it to what happens during a hurricane when the eye passes overhead. At first, there is a lot of rain, high wind, thunder and lightning. Things which are not secured are probably blowing around. The whole scene is very chaotic. Then everything gets calm and the sky clears. You might get tricked into believing that the storm has subsided all together. However, this lull is deceptive and lasts for only a short time. Those who are wise will not fall for this deception. They remain focused, because they understand that the worst is yet to come.

If you have any doubt about the ability of *the Chaos Cohorts* to make use of redirection, consider how the confusion and drama generated by the event which follows more than served to redirect attention away from how the President was handling (or not handling) the health care situation (and many other matters) in this country. The media had a field day, telling and retelling the details.

The date was October 4, 2017. The debate on Capitol Hill about health care and tax reform was hot and heavy. The President, as usual, was under fire. Then, we got the news about four young American soldiers being ambushed and killed during a raid in a country in Africa. Our president, the moral leader of this country, waited for twelve days after the incident before speaking to the nation about this tragedy.

The deaths of those soldiers gave "Gold Star" status to their families. Three of the soldiers were Caucasian. One of the soldiers was a young African American man. His grieving widow (24-years old, mother of their two children and pregnant with their third child), received a telephone call from the President while driving to an airport to be present as her husband's body was returned to our country.

The telephone conversation was overheard by their state representative, also an African American woman, who was traveling in the car with this young wife and family members. This state representative had a long-standing personal relationship with the family and had mentored the deceased soldier. As it turns out, the conversation was also overheard by people in the room at the White House with the President while he was talking. The state representative reported that the young widow took offense at the words used by the President while making reference to her deceased husband. It is not known what words were used when consoling the other widows. The accuracy of this report, as stated by the state representative, was supported by the mother of the deceased soldier. The mother said that her son had been "disrespected" by what the President said. It was reported that the young widow became visibly distraught, and stated that the President did not know her name or the name of her deceased husband.

The state representative shared what happened with members of the media. After this conversation was made public, the matter unfortunately descended to the disgusting level of an elementary school yard "he-said, she-said" cat-fight, with no positive resolution in sight. The President and members of the White House Staff accused the state representative of grandstanding, lying, and making a private matter public. The state representative accused the President of launching a personal attack upon her, lying and attempting to damage her reputation as an elected official. She has since received death threats for coming forward with the story.

The worst thing about it was that a grieving family was denied the support needed as they prepared for a memorial service. A great deal of media time, at least for a few days, was dedicated to what amounted to coverage of a living soap-opera, complete with melodrama, a cast of characters, and emotional turmoil. There was no time left for discussion about anything else. The President was given a "break" from defending his stance on other issues, like those related to health care in this country. Bravo.

CHAPTER 26
The Eye of the Hurricane

With the passing of time, the media is once again slowly revisiting the status of health care in this country. The politicians and the experts have center stage and are making plans concerning what the official policy will eventually become.

Concerns as to the fair and impartial application of the prior authorization process makes this the perfect time, especially for caregivers, to outline goals and plan strategy. *The Chaos Cohorts* are working overtime, possibly to come up with another strategy to redirect our attention while they pursue their self-serving agendas. We are in the eye of the hurricane. The importance of not getting caught-up in distractions cannot be understated, because that is how the best problem- solving and decision making efforts get derailed.

Although plans are being made to eventually repeal or revise the *Patient Protection and Affordable Care Act*, it looks like it will remain in place for now. This is the U.S. healthcare reform law, implemented during the administration of former President Barack Obama in March of 2010.

A basic feature of the *Patient Protection and Affordable Care Act* is that everybody will have healthcare, even if it means that a lot of money in the form of subsidies will go to help people falling into certain income groups. This money comes from sources such as higher taxes being paid by Americans in higher income brackets, and from more taxes placed on biopharmaceutical companies.

Our President supports people being able to cross state lines to purchase lower cost health care plans, and also to increase the number of options people have to do business with. He supports the use of subsidies, but (at this time) he wants this money to come from the federal government in the form of block grants. States getting these block grants could use this money as they desired, meaning that some people might not get as much coverage as they need (if any). This could put health insurance companies at a disadvantage, but not for long, because the federal government could undermine the authority of the individual state. Remember that health insurance companies are controlled by <u>federal</u> statutes which set broad policy and approve budgets, as well as by state laws and regulations. The powers that be at the federal government level could obstruct those state health insurance rules which they don't approve of.

Perhaps the issue is not only one of quantity, but <u>quality</u>. Having several health insurance companies to choose from is important, because it prevents monopolies.

There is another action which should be included, but is not being addressed. Now is the time to make sure that these companies use processes, such as prior authorization, in a way that acts in the best interest of patients.

What does having more health care insurance company options matter in the absence of discussion about how to end the misuse and abuse of strategies, like the prior authorization process? We need the process to change so that barriers limiting access to pharmaceutical drugs requiring medical prescriptions no longer exist. The reason that I buy health care insurance is so that I can access (at some future date) what the medical world has to offer in order to either save my life, or improve the quality of my life. I enter into that deal thinking that decisions made by all involved are going to be in my favor, as long as they are based upon legitimate requests and hard data. I do not pay money for last minute surprises or disappointments when I am suffering and in need of assistance. That's it. End of story.

As far as the prior authorization process goes, the opinion of my doctor/practitioner (a representative of my choice) who recommends a pharmaceutical drug, based upon history with my case and supportive data, should be considered. It matters. This is especially true for those which my doctor/practitioner deems "medically necessary." I would venture to guess that I am not alone in questioning whether or not a health insurance company, which uses a process as a strategy to create barriers which keeps this from happening, is working on my behalf.

When all is said and done, change can't happen until federal agencies write and approve laws and regulations, and then put them into effect. It's just a matter of time, and the clock is ticking. I would venture to guess that *the Chaos Cohorts* know this, and are using this time to their advantage. It would be interesting to find out just how much money biopharmaceutical companies contribute to congressional lobbying, funding and campaign efforts. The "pay to play" approach is something that *the Chaos Cohorts* would appreciate. The question is, what are we doing?

II – THE PROFIT

CHAPTER 27
What's in Your Chocolates?

I can predict when I'm going to have a bad day. My first telephone call comes from a fast-talking "slickster" of a salesperson, trying to deceive me into buying something that I don't need. I try to hang the telephone up as soon as possible, but sometimes not soon enough to avoid getting that queasy feeling in the pit of my stomach. My husband and I worked and saved for many years so that we could enjoy the good things in life. It seems like you can never let your guard down, because someone is always waiting to make a profit at your expense.

These slicksters may attempt to disguise their voices so as not to be obvious. However, what these people are really after soon gives them away. As a group, they all use similar tactics. They are disruptive, take up too much of my time, and want personal information that could compromise my credit status. They are definitely not trustworthy. They try hard to persuade me to buy their products, usually without reading the fine print. Each one tries to convince me that he/she is my best friend and knows what's best for me.

Sound familiar? It should, because these are the tactics used by *the Chaos Cohorts* – biopharmaceutical companies, health insurance companies, distributors (pharmacy benefit management companies and wholesale drug distributors) and the federal government. All of them have the same goal. They want to get as much money from you as quickly as possible, giving as little as possible in return, without your realizing it or taking steps to do anything about it.

These companies have mastered how to use "key" tactics or tools, to successfully distract you while they accomplish their own objectives. When it comes to health care, the prior authorization process is fare game. They know how to get you to make decisions based entirely upon emotions, rather than logical thinking. If you are able to catch onto what they are doing, it's often too late to do anything about it.

That queasy feeling in my gut that I get when those fast-talking slickster salespeople call is what I now get when dealing with agents of *the Chaos Cohorts*. At this point in time, my sole reason for dealing with them is to help my husband, Walt, get prior authorization approval for the only life-saving pharmaceutical drug in existence which will help him manage his bad LDL cholesterol.

I don't remember ever going through anything like this before Walt needed this medication. My first interaction with the health care system was as a child, and certainly not like this. I lived in a segregated, urban part of a large city in a Southern state. As was true of the times, African American patients could only be seen by African American doctors/practitioners. My memories were framed by pleasant interactions with doctors/practitioners who were friendly, encouraging, patient, trustworthy and respectful. The enjoyment they had for their work was shown during interactions with their patients. These healing angels went out of their way, and to the best of their ability, to help patients who were sick and suffering.

When I was a child and got sick, my mother or grandmother would make one telephone call to our family doctor/practitioner. I remember that my doctor/practitioner was a very kind man who always wore a suit, carried a big black bag full of "weird" looking instruments, and had something draped around his neck that looked to my "child" eyes like a snake.

No matter how sick I was, I could somehow get to the living room window to watch my doctor/practitioner as he drove his car up to our house and walked to our front door. Then, I would go into my act. I would whine, demand attention and run around the house (which made me feel worse). My doctor/practitioner, my healing angel, had the patience of Job. (Job was an honorable and wealthy man who suffered much personal misfortune, but never lost faith in God.) Although he was polite, he would not pay much attention to me until my annoying behavior subsided. At some point, I would become tired and settle down. It was then that he would interact so kindly with me, and make me feel so special, that I felt like I was princess of the universe.

His actions made me feel that the reason for his very existence was to help me get better. His treatment plan for me included calling me by my nickname and telling funny jokes, which always made me smile and laugh. As my behavior became more civilized, he was able to ask me questions about how I felt and take my temperature. I trusted him, because he never gave me a reason not to do so.

He would talk with my mother and grandmother about how to make me comfortable, and even ask them how they were holding-up. In return, they would ask him if he wanted something to eat. This offer was never refused. The rest of the visit was devoted to gossip about what was happening in the neighborhood, as all of our neighbors were also his patients.

We did not have health insurance, because there was no need. My doctor would charge a fee for his services, and he would be paid. The fees which he charged were comparable to those charged by other doctors/practitioners in our community, and were reasonable. We could afford to pay them out-of-pocket. In that sense, my doctor/practitioner acted as my insurance company. If I needed to see a specialist for some reason, my doctor/practitioner would make a referral. He managed each of his cases, with the specialists sending their reports to him. He had one nurse working with him. This allowed him to do the work that he loved, and kept his one-man practice open at the same time.

His visits always included leaving a prescription for some kind of awful tasting red or yellow- colored liquid medicine. My mother would take the prescription to our neighborhood pharmacy. The pharmacist never questioned my doctors/practitioners judgment, and always filled it promptly. I took the medicine without question, because I trusted my doctor/practitioner. Even though I didn't care for the medicine or shots he gave me, I knew that I would always feel better at some point. I had confidence in him, because he never let me down.

What I remember most is that he never left our home without giving me "chocolates." I knew that he carried a few pieces in his big black bag. I also knew that I would only get some if I didn't cause him too much aggravation. Otherwise, he would just leave, telling me goodbye on the way out.

In a way, we had an unspoken contract. Chocolates served as a pacifier. The knowledge that I would receive them as payment for something that I chose to do was additional motivation for me to settle down. In a way, "being good" was the price that I agreed to pay for those chocolates.

I never worried about the quality of the chocolates, because I knew that he was not going to hurt me. The look of pure joy on his face when he saw how happy I was to get that pacifier left no doubt as to the sincerity of his motives. I swore that I was going to marry him when I grew up. Of course, we would live in the fantasy city of Caring.

CHAPTER 28
Wealth Defined

The great thing about pleasant memories is having something pleasant to look back on, especially when things go wrong. Pleasant memories help you keep things light when the dark side is too heavy. I am fortunate, because I had many positive experiences with my childhood doctor/practitioner, which now fall into that category. I know that the doctor/practitioner of my childhood years, and Walt's nephrologist (our shining star) would have gotten along well.

Now that I am an adult, I understand that people have needs which they will try to satisfy. One of those needs is to be productive and useful in one way or another. Working, along with rewards earned, is a way to satisfy this need. People work for different reasons. People will work for money so that they can buy things that are wanted or needed. People will also work because they like the feeling of accomplishment that goes with obtaining objectives.

It's a wonderful thing when your work is something that you love and enjoy doing. I am sure that the doctor/practitioner of my childhood years would fall into this category. There were many ways in which he received payment for his services. He received money on a fee - for - service basis. He received delicious meals and Southern hospitality. He also received positive feedback from me, because his actions helped me feel better. I am sure that this made him feel happy that his efforts had not been in vain.

Based upon his storehouse of knowledge and experience, my doctor/practitioner picked the best strategy to use for a given situation. He tested that strategy with me and those around me and received confirmation that it worked. There was no need to change anything. I bought into it and altered my behavior accordingly. In effect, we had all of the elements of an unspoken contract. Changing the strategy would have called for renegotiating a new contract. The price that I paid to earn those chocolates did not harm me or cause any problems. In return, receiving those chocolates made me a "very" happy camper.

My doctor/practitioner determined how much to charge for his services. During that time period, entities like *the Chaos Cohorts* had yet to acquire the power, control, and influence over the medical world that they have today. Crippling governmental distractions had yet to come on the scene. My doctor/practitioner used a sliding-scale fee method, which worked for him and his patients. Higher income patients paid more, and lower income patients paid less. Patients within both income groups received the same excellent quality of service delivery.

I expect that the healing angel of my childhood days, my doctor/practitioner, has by this time gone on to greener pastures. His approach to money collection did not make him financially wealthy while on this earth. But, I like to think that his charitable and giving nature ensured a well-deserved spot in heaven, where I hear that the streets are paved with pure gold.

CHAPTER 29
The High Cost of Pacifiers

The wonderful doctor/practitioner of my childhood would certainly be amazed (and probably upset) by how things have evolved over the years. With increasing power, control and influence, *the Chaos Cohorts* have changed the health care service scene in this country from one of "pacifying patients" to "pacifying themselves."

The days when a doctor/practitioner could act as a patient's health insurance company are long gone. Health care coverage today is too often provided by impersonal, paper-pushing bureaucrats. These entities work for health care companies that take a percentage off the top from the money we pay to them. We allow them to control our money until we need services, and then they frequently betray our trust. These entities are known as health insurance companies. They are branches of *the Chaos Cohorts*.

Health insurance companies don't know us as individuals and there is no personal contact. They make life and death decisions concerning what should happen to us, and they get away with it. It's sad, but true, that patients are more likely to frame encounters with the health care system of today by frustration, anger, disappointment, apathy, cold-heartedness, mistrust, deception and greed.

Do doctors/practitioners still make home visits? I personally don't know of any who do. As far as the "chocolates" go, I know of few instances where you actually get what you thought that you bargained and paid for. If you get any offers, it's best to question where they are coming from and what's in them before you rush to eat them. Ingredients unknown to you might be in there, which could make you sick, hate the taste, or kill you.

The patient of today who needs health care intervention is more likely to experience the following series of events. You go to the doctor's/practitioner's office, usually after making a telephone call and almost begging someone with a monotone voice for an "as soon as possible" appointment.

In the meantime, and if you are really feeling ill, you are advised to go to the emergency room of the hospital closest to where you are at the time. You make the trip either driving yourself, by ambulance, or with someone driving you. Once there, you are greeted by a sign (not a person) which directs you to a "kiosk" so that you can type-in your health insurance information. Hopefully, your eye-hand coordination is still intact, along with your ability to focus. Pray for divine intervention if you have no health insurance or if your insurance will not cover the kind of hospitalization services that you will ultimately receive (for example, outpatient, inpatient, or observational).

Someone at a desk will finally realize that you are in the room and take your vitals. When you actually get seen for a more in-depth screening will depend upon their perception of how sick you are (on a scale of 1 to 10). This is a process known as "triage." It helps to really act like you truly feel, rather than toughing it out.

Vitals will be taken; then, you will usually go back into the waiting room or to get labs drawn. In the meantime, you are being exposed to all of the germs brought into the environment by other patients. Don't be afraid to ask for a face mask. Your immune system, which is probably already compromised, will thank you. Then you go into another area and wait some more, maybe take a nap. It's usually around that time that a decision is made whether to consider you as "outpatient" (go home that same day), "inpatient" (admit you into the hospital for a longer stay), or "observational" (a kind of outpatient "limbo-like world" status where you are not technically on inpatient status but end up spending more than one day and night in the hospital).

If you see your doctor/practitioner during an office visit, you will most likely wait for what seems like hours in a room barren of amenities, with the exception of wall posters and brochures advertising various drugs. The room temperature is usually just above freezing. Someone will come in, tell you to take off your clothes and put on a paper-thin or cloth gown. You wait some more, maybe take a nap. The nurse or physician's assistant comes in, asks a few questions (which you have already answered), and leaves. Again, you wait for what seems like hours in the room barren of amenities, with the exception of wall posters and brochures advertising various drugs.

Finally, the doctor/practitioner comes in, starts entering more data into a laptop computer or a tape- recorder, and maybe checks x-rays (if taken) displayed on a monitor. If you are really lucky, the doctor/practitioner gives you about fifteen minutes (give or take) of his/her time. Then maybe you get a prescription for medication or a referral for more tests. If the medication works, you may or may not have a follow-up visit. Otherwise, you will most likely be scheduled for a follow-up visit if more tests are involved or symptoms persist. In the event of a follow-up visit, you will find yourself starting at the beginning of this scenario as you repeat the above process. Oh happy day!

CHAPTER 30
Deal Breaker Aftershocks

Neither Walt nor I can remember when the focus of health care in the United States changed from "patients" to "big business profit margins." The last thing that patients, caregivers or doctors/practitioners need to worry about is whether or not there is anything in health care insurance contracts concerning promises, payment, or reimbursement for services rendered, that will not be honored by health insurance companies as expected.

I'll have to admit that I have mixed feelings about the motives of doctors/practitioners. Honestly, when it comes to greed and broken promises, patients and doctors/practitioners seem to be in the same boat. Both patients and doctors/practitioners take turns as victims. The victimizer of both groups is usually the health insurance company, a branch of *the Chaos Cohorts*.

As a patient, you purchase a health insurance plan and enter into a contract with a health insurance company. Do you always read the small print? If you do, do you really understand what you are reading?

When you visit your doctors/practitioners office, can you honestly say that you read all of the notices positioned on the sign-in counter, especially if you are sick, running late, or if there is a line of people behind you waiting to sign in?

There are many consequences for a patient who fails to obey health plan contractual expectations. Most health insurance companies charge patients some kind of monthly premium. What would be the consequence if you failed to pay on time? You might be allowed some kind of a specified time period to make things right. I'll bet that your coverage ends if your payment is not made before the end of that period.

A similar fate might await a patient who consistently fails to make timely co-payments (co-pays) to his/her doctor/practitioner. In order to assist you, a compassionate doctor/practitioner might offer a payment plan, or make a compromise on a one-time basis. However, you probably won't get another appointment with that doctor/practitioner.

In the event that you continue to not make your co-pays, your name will most likely be sent to a collection agency. You might get a number of dunning telephone calls at home and at work. Your credit score will definitely suffer and impact future purchasing power. The bottom line is that you will probably be in for major headaches.

Times are hard for many people, especially where money is concerned. Some people have to make difficult choices, like whether to eat or pay for medications. If this happened to me as a patient or caregiver of a patient, I would most likely feel persecuted or sorry for myself, and try my best to find someone else to blame for my predicament.

As it pertains to my doctor/practitioner, my first reaction would be to label him/her as uncaring, and blame him/her for not appreciating my position. After calming myself down, I would realize that the doctor/practitioner is not the true culprit. Those who are really to blame and stand to profit the most (the health care insurance company) don't care about what anyone else is going through. They just want money and will do whatever is necessary to get it, no matter who gets hurt in the process.

Every coin has two sides. Doctors/practitioners probably make more money than most of us could ever imagine. In spite of their economic status, they are not granted immunity from being on the losing end of the deal. As has happened with patients, actions taken by *the Chaos Cohorts* have affected the lives of doctors/practitioners in many ways.

Health insurance companies are quick to call patients to task for suspected non-compliance. Do doctors/practitioners who write insurance contracts with health insurance companies enjoy the same privilege? Logic would dictate that these professionals expect health insurance companies to be accountable for their actions, unless their deal is actually one-sided.

It is a well known fact that there is no love lost between them, because doctors/practitioners feel (and are often) powerless when it comes to dealing with health insurance companies. Conversations with Walt's doctors/practitioners reveals that it's dealing with the bureaucracy that gets to them, which shows- up in the form of stress, depression, and generally feeling burned-out.

By now, you know that I ask a lot of questions. I especially like to do this when talking with Walt's doctors/practitioners. I learn a lot from them and they seem to appreciate the opportunity to talk to someone who will listen to their concerns. Did you know, for example, that some doctors/practitioners are not renewing their contracts with health insurance companies, because those health insurance companies want them to accept less money as providers? Accepting less money as providers would mean that more would go to the health insurance company.

Did you know that a health insurance company can penalize a doctor/practitioner if patients don't make co-payments? Doctors/practitioners who are employed by a facility (for example, nursing home or hospital) get paid by that facility. The facility assumes the responsibility when patients don't pay for services; however, the doctor/practitioner may receive a salary cut.

Doctors/practitioners in private practice would also have a hard way to go if patients did not meet co-pays. Some doctors/practitioners may feel charitable or compassionate, and sometimes wave co-pays for one or two visits (for example, a military family, economic hardships, or homeless). However, doctors/practitioners working in these settings have contracts with health insurance companies, and those companies can impose a number of negative consequences when they waive patient co-pays, to include charges of fraud, contract violation, and sanctions. Not to worry. It's just that master (controller) - slave (obeys the controller) thing.

CHAPTER 31
Coding is King

The medical practice of a doctor/practitioner is his/her business. When it comes to health care, we no longer live in a country with a fee - for- service health care payment model. These professionals are due payment for services rendered, because it takes money to run a medical practice. Have you ever wondered how fees are determined? Are there some activities which are expected, but for which a doctor/practitioner will not get reimbursed? Enter the health insurance company, a charter member of *the Chaos Cohorts*.

There was a time when only two parties were involved in a health care transaction: doctors/practitioners and their patients. The doctor/practitioner kept paper medical records and acted as a health insurance company for his/her patient. Patients got the prescription medications recommended by these professionals, because the doctor/practitioner was considered to be the expert. Walt certainly remembers this happening when he was a child. I know that the doctor/practitioner of my childhood years followed this practice.

I remember that my doctor/practitioner kept a notebook, and that he would take a few minutes during each visit to write in that notebook before he left our home. That was back when times were simpler. Entities like *the Chaos Cohorts* had yet to acquire the power that they have today to dictate and administer policies and procedures.

Today, there are three main players involved in health care scenarios: the patient (gets the medical service), the provider (doctor/practitioner), and the payer (for example, a health insurance company). When you think about it, it all boils down to partnerships and contracts. The residents of the fantasy city of Chaos would be content and find no problem with this.

A patient contracts with a health insurance company so that he/she can receive services in the event that assistance is needed at some point in the future. Doctors/practitioners also make contracts with health insurance companies which include how much they expect to be paid for their services. Things can get complicated unless there is some way to keep track of all of the details. That way is through the use of electronic technology.

All of Walt's doctors/practitioners, without exception, agree that they would be unable to run their practices without the use of electronic technology. This includes the use of electronic medical record systems (EMR systems). These systems provide convenient access to patient information, are almost indestructible, and save time.

I don't know of any doctor/practitioner who fails to make use of a lap- top computer on a regular basis. Lap-top computers are a form of electronic technology, and their use is a common practice. They serve a variety of purposes, such as to keep summary notes, create electronic charts, and send prescription medication orders to pharmacies.

The use of electronic technology helps when it comes time to calculate how much money doctors/practitioners get paid. Doctors/practitioners work with medical coders and medical billers for this purpose. Medical coders and medical billers work together to create claims. Medical billers, in addition to working with medical coders, check to make sure that claims have all of the details which are needed to determine reimbursement rates.

Every visit with a doctor/practitioner ends with a staff member giving a patient a form (usually pink or yellow) to take to the check-out window. A close review of that form reveals various codes matched to services/procedures which provide specific information needed for billing purposes. These codes are created to communicate information. They are a kind of shorthand, which stand for something that has meaning to those who need to know. They are a requirement and are submitted to the health insurance company as part of a medical claim.

Claims which reach the health insurance company are reviewed to make sure that they are complete. Then a decision is made regarding if payment is due and how much money the doctor/practitioner will get. There are three possible outcomes: approval, denial or outright rejection.

Even when a claim is approved, expectations of doctors/practitioners may differ from those of health insurance companies regarding how much they will be paid. The health insurance company might use different payment amounts than those which the doctor/practitioner expects.

Following a decision, the medical biller prepares a statement for the patient. This statement is the bill for services received. It represents what the doctor/practitioner did and what was approved by the health insurance company. The medical biller also makes sure that the patient is notified, explains benefits and follows-up in cases of delinquency.

A common frustration among doctors/practitioners is that there are some activities for which they will not get reimbursed by the health insurance company.

A claim might be denied, for example, if the doctor/practitioner bills for a procedure that is not included in the patients contract, such as a non- approved pre-existing condition. If rejected, then the doctor/practitioner can initiate an appeal process with the health insurance company. This is where having good karma might prove helpful!

Another frustration among doctors/practitioners is that they will not get reimbursed by the health insurance company for the amount of time spent completing paperwork required by the prior authorization process.

In Walt's case, his doctor/practitioner (nephrologist) spent a great deal of time and energy responding to various clinical assessment questions included in paperwork required for the prior authorization process. He would not be reimbursed by the health insurance company for any of this work, regardless of whether approval was given or denied. It was required by the health insurance company due to his recommendation regarding the most appropriate pharmaceutical drug for Walt to take.

The bottom line is that health insurance companies (branches of *the Chaos Cohorts*) victimize patients and medical professionals. They tell doctors/practitioners what to do, how to do it, and what they will get for doing it. They expect doctors/practitioners to do extra work without compensation. They pay a set amount for certain types of procedures and want to keep their costs as low as possible. Health insurance companies benefit monetarily by negotiating contracts with doctors/practitioners to their own advantage whenever possible. They act as though they are all-powerful, because they have been allowed to do so. Omnipotence is often associated with being "god-like." I have no doubt that this status is one which health insurance companies see themselves as possessing. It wouldn't be too hard to make a comparison between the agenda of their counterparts in the fantasy city of Chaos and what is actually happening in the real world in which we live. I wonder if they realize (or even care) how hard the fall from Mount Olympus might be.

CHAPTER 32
What's for Dinner?

The quest for "god-like" status is not limited to being something that only individual people desire. Groups, organizations, and agencies also pursue this goal and hunger for whatever reward they can get. The acquisition of profit is the "ambrosia and nectar" of *the Chaos Cohorts*. They go after it with all of the passion befitting their self-appointed god-like status, and our bank accounts seem to be the main course on their dinner menus.

Biopharmaceutical companies, health insurance companies, and distributors (for example, pharmacy benefit management companies, PBM's), have been allowed to use strategies such as the prior authorization process to make a dollar at our expense. Their efforts have been aided and abetted by our own government. Their disregard of what a doctor/practitioner prescribes reeks of arrogance, undermines the authority of the doctor/practitioner, discriminates, and may well act as a barrier to patients seeking rightful access to life-saving pharmaceutical drugs requiring medical prescriptions. Biopharmaceutical companies, health insurance companies, and distributors (such as pharmacy benefit management companies, PBM's) do what they do in order to make money. Wouldn't it be great if we had the power to say "no" to their dinner invitation?

CHAPTER 33:
True Colors Will Show

Biopharmaceutical companies (branches of *the Chaos Cohorts*) play critical roles in the life of pharmaceutical drugs requiring medical prescriptions. These companies make the drugs and set the first prices. It is not unheard of for these prices to change before the medications get to patients, pharmacies or doctors/practitioners.

Once produced, decisions are made regarding how these drugs will reach patients. Distribution is handled by an entity of *the Chaos Cohorts* which has a kind of split personality, because it's made-up of two components: wholesale drug distributors and pharmacy benefit management company's (PBM's). The personality shown depends upon the tasks required.

Biopharmaceutical companies use pharmacy benefit management companies (PBM's), and their agents (pharmaceutical/ sales representatives), when marketing drugs which require medical prescriptions to pharmacies and doctors/practitioners.

Pharmacy benefit management companies (PBM's) act as "go-betweens" (middle-men), between the biopharmaceutical company and the health insurance company. They handle activities such as reviewing requests for medications, managing prescriptions, and formularies and claims adjustments.

Health insurance companies love low drug prices. In fact, the lower, the better. PBM's are hired to make this happen. They negotiate to get what they consider to be the best treatment for the lowest cost. Theoretically, there is nothing wrong with this, if it is in the patient's best interest. If these companies "rubber stamp" recommendations made by health insurance and biopharmaceutical companies, which compromise the health and well being of patients to satisfy their own needs (for example, profit margins, power, control), they show their true colors as branches of *the Chaos Cohorts*. It becomes appropriate to question exactly whose interests they are actually concerned about (in addition to their own). What happened to Walt during his prior authorization process serves as a good example of how this can work to the detriment of a patient.

Walt's doctor/practitioner (nephrologist) requested that the prior authorization process be started in order to grant legitimate access to the pharmaceutical drug needed to control his bad LDL cholesterol. A pharmacy benefit management company (PBM) worked with Walt's health insurance company. The two entities got together and decided that the PBM company would assume the leadership role regarding decisions about acceptance or denial of the request. The doctor/practitioner (nephrologist) sent information to the health insurance company. The health insurance company sent this information to the PBM.

Walt appointed his doctor/practitioner (nephrologist) to act as his representative. This appointment was made for two reasons: (1) his nephrologist prescribed the drug in question; and, (2) they had a long and positive medical relationship, based upon mutual trust and respect. It was his nephrologist who completed and submitted all paperwork required by the health insurance company, and emphasized the need to expedite approval due to medical reasons. He never received a dime for all of the work that he did or the time that he spent. His doctor/practitioner (nephrologist) did this because Walt needed to have access to the only drug which would control his bad LDL cholesterol. Managing his bad LDL cholesterol would assist with the treatment of his kidney disease.

A subsequent letter was sent by the PBM company to Walt's doctor/practitioner (nephrologist), who then forwarded a copy to Walt. In that letter, it was stated that: (1) sufficient information had not been provided to establish coverage of the requested medication under the health care insurance plan, (2) Walt did not have one of the three required medical conditions (he really does have one of them but couldn't find a cardiologist willing to put this in writing), and (3) the doctor/practitioner requesting the medication was not practicing in one of the specialty areas sanctioned by the health insurance company (see Appendix P, Letter dated March 8, 2017). This rationale was upheld for a second time during an appeal process (see Appendix Q, Letter dated June 7, 2017). The health insurance company supported the decision made by the pharmacy benefit management company (PBM). Now, take a deep breath, count from 1 to 10, exhale, and try to relax.

Another way that biopharmaceutical companies market prescription medications (and over-the-counter drugs) to doctor/practitioners and pharmacies is through wholesale drug distributors. This is especially true when dealing with community pharmacies. As is true for PBM companies, wholesale drug distributors employ sales representatives who deliver pharmaceutical drugs requiring medical prescriptions to pharmacies and doctors/practitioners, and over-the-counter drugs to pharmacies.

As is true of anyone making a living in the sales industry, income and job security depend on how much you sell. Wholesale distribution companies are in business to make money. When wholesale distribution companies partner with health care insurance companies, patients, once again, can frequently get the short end of the stick. I am going to digress for a moment, because I want to share the following example of how I made this discovery the hard way.

A pharmacy benefit company (PBM) sales representative paid a visit to one of Walt's doctors/practitioners. A brand name medication (pro-biotic dietary supplement) was introduced to the doctor/practitioner, and the doctor/practitioner subsequently gave free samples to Walt. The medication did an excellent job of controlling one of the many conditions that Walt has. In fact, it was so helpful that we asked that a prescription be sent to Walt's health insurance company so that he could get the medication on a regular basis.

Within a few days, we received a letter from the health care insurance company, stating that they were not going to pay for the supplement as a prescription medication. Their reason was that it was available as an "over the counter supplement." Ok, I'll buy that (no pun intended). Upon paying a visit to our community pharmacy, I was told that it was not in stock, but could be ordered.

The wholesale distribution company supplying the pro-biotic as a drug supplement had it in their formulary.

Remember that I ask a lot of questions. I decided to conduct my own investigation which consisted of walking around the store and comparing prices of other pro-biotic supplements which were already on the shelves. I was especially interested in brand name pro-biotic (drug) supplements sold in 30-day quantities which would be the same quantity as the prescription written by Walt's doctor/practitioner. My investigation revealed that the average price per bottle for a 30-day supply of brand name pro-biotic (drug) supplements (already on the shelves) ranged from approximately $9.00 to $20.00. The average cost per pill ranged from approximately five cents to $1.10.

When I returned to the pharmacy counter, I was told that the cost for a 30-day supply of the brand name pro-biotic dietary supplement recommended by Walt's doctor/practitioner (as a prescription) was about $1.50 per pill. Again, that was the cost, per pill. Let's do the math. Twelve months in a year, average of 30-days per month. That totals approximately $45 per month, or $540 per year (before taxes). Sounds like inflation to me. I can't help but wonder what it really costs to make one of these pills. Unfortunately, I was unable to find any information to share with you regarding such a cost. Apparently patients and caregivers are "out of the loop" when it comes to this information.

CHAPTER 34
Emissaries and Their Trappings

Everyone wants to be compensated in one form or another for the things that they do for others. Business owners generally do what they do in order to make money. The doctor/practitioner of my childhood years used a sliding scale fee - for- service system. There was no doubt that this represented the lion's share of his income. He also enjoyed plenty of good food and Southern hospitality during those house calls, especially around holiday seasons.

In many respects, the doctors/practitioners of today probably aren't that different. Those I know seem to be pretty well off, financially speaking. While there may be some out there, I don't know of any who make house calls anymore. I imagine that they find various ways to amass their fortunes. Being able to make good deals when it comes to purchasing drugs is probably a strategy that helps this happen.

Most people know that doctors/practitioners prescribe and administer a variety of pharmaceutical drugs requiring medical prescriptions. Dealing with pharmacy benefit management companies (PBM's) is one way that doctors/practitioners get access to these drugs. They buy these from pharmacy benefit management companies (PBM's), and then negotiate with the health insurance company for reimbursement. PBM's buy their prescription medications from biopharmaceutical companies.

Health insurance companies love low drug prices. In fact, the lower, the better. Pharmacy benefit managers (PBM's) look for drugs that will best manage problematic health conditions for the lowest price. What happens when there are conflicts between keeping costs low, concern for patient benefit, and recommendations made by doctors/practitioners? Consider Walt's case as an example.

The pharmaceutical drug that Walt needs to control his bad LDL cholesterol is one of the most expensive prescription medications on the market today. It's given by injection, every other week. It can't be found on the shelves of any neighborhood pharmacy, because only a few specialized pharmacies make it. Prior authorization approval is needed to qualify and pay for it, and it's sent to patients through the mail.

During a prior chapter, I mentioned that Walt had gone to several cardiologists in an attempt to find one who would have enough professional integrity to advocate for him so that he could get this medication. The third cardiologist in this chain of specialists continuously made reference to the fact that, along with everything else, Walt probably would not qualify for the medication because it was "very expensive." Health insurance companies generally don't want to pay for expensive medications. Maybe this was his way of telling us that the biopharmaceutical companies, health insurance companies, and PBM's had already come to an agreement that this drug would be available to only a select segment of the larger patient population. Did they forget about all of the other patients who couldn't take statin drugs, but still needed to control their skyrocketing bad LDL cholesterol levels? Did they ever care?

It's important to read your health insurance plan paperwork. Notice that health insurance companies have lists of pharmaceutical drugs which they will and will not pay for. PBM's oversee these lists, which are known as formularies. There are many, many drugs on the market today. It seems as though some drugs get placed on these lists and some do not. Some require prior authorization approval and some are over-the-counter.

A bottle of aspirin serves as a good example. There are many reasons why people use aspirin, such as: to reduce fever, pain and swelling; or, relieve headaches. Community stores do not discriminate. They accept money from anyone who wants to purchase this drug. Anybody can go into a pharmacy (or store) and purchase a bottle of aspirin. Several brands are right there on the shelves within easy reach. Needless to say, aspirin will probably be around for at least a few more years. The cost may differ, depending upon whether your choice is generic or brand name.

Now, when was the last time you needed a prescription from a doctor/practitioner certifying medical necessity as a requirement for buying a little bottle of aspirin (generic or brand name), let alone prior authorization approval from your health insurance company or PBM intervention.

Both Walt and I remember that at some point we heard about something called prior authorization. When we compared our notes, we agreed that this was around the time when doctors/practitioners started prescribing drugs which were a little more pricy, and perhaps had no generic equivalent. These drugs had no coupons available for discounts, and maybe required a more "interesting" administration method (for example, injection versus oral).

Another tactic used by biopharmaceutical companies is to hire people to work as liaisons between themselves and the doctors/practitioners. These people are known as pharmaceutical (drug) sales representatives. They introduce drugs to doctors/practitioners with the intent of getting them to buy from them. Sales representatives are usually working for a wholesaler who has gotten the drug from the biopharmaceutical company. How many times have you had to wait to see your own doctor/practitioner until the drug company sales representative has finished making a sales pitch? My experience has been that they just go to the check-in window and present a business card – all on a walk-in basis. Never mind it that you had a set appointment time, maybe booked weeks in advance.

While it's probably not the lion's share of their income, conversations with other caregivers (and my own observations as a patient or when accompanying my husband to medical appointments) reveals that we have all witnessed those pharmaceutical sales (drug company) representatives, passing through waiting rooms, wheeling luggage carriers overflowing with boxes and suitcases of every size, as they disappear into back offices.

I have often wondered what's in those suitcases, especially in light of the posters and advertisements on the walls of just about every examination room. There are many drugs on the market today. However, posters that I have seen seem to only advertise a few brand name medications. Looking at them gives me a déjà vu feeling, almost like I'm watching television commercials advertising the latest and greatest pill to cure what troubles you. I can't help but wonder if this is why doctors/practitioners keep such a large supply of paper rolls for those examination room tables. Could it be that frequent changes of that paper are needed to remove all of the blood spilled by drug representatives fighting each other for the right to display their trappings? That's a topic for another book.

CHAPTER 35
The Power of Knowing

Both Walt and I are children of God. Having said this, I often find myself wondering what the world would be like if Jesus would come back and abolish all sickness and disease.

Jesus didn't reject anyone who wanted to be healed. He didn't charge money. This would definitely create problems for all branches of *the Chaos Cohorts*. A lot of people would have to rethink ways of making a living. Health care professionals, for example, like doctors/practitioners, would immediately be put out of business. Biopharmaceutical companies, health insurance companies, and distributors (pharmacy benefit management companies, PBM's) and wholesale distributors) would have to find new ways of profit-making, which they now do at the expense of people who are sick and suffering, because there would be none.

Whatever happened to the power to heal that was given to the twelve disciples of Jesus? Given everything else they have done, it's not unreasonable to infer that *the Chaos Cohorts* stopped the tradition of teaching each new generation of disciples healing powers. Just think about the multitude of healers that would be here on Earth today if every generation, from the time when Jesus lived to today, had continued to produce a minimum of twelve disciples gifted with the power to heal. Since this does not appear to have happened to date, entities such as biopharmaceutical companies, health insurance companies, and distributors have been more than willing to fill the gap.

I would love to live long enough to see his return. Jesus only asked that people believe in him and have faith that he was making commitments to do what he said he would do. His disciples had absolute faith in him. That was why they were able to follow him and endure hardships. This is what having faith is all about. It's more than what you can hear, see, touch, smell, or taste. It's about understanding the difference between "know-ing" and "no-ing." Wouldn't that be something special?

CHAPTER 36
Knowing or No-ing? That is the Question

Walt is the owner of his own company, <u>Development of Relaxation Powers</u>, where he teaches self-hypnosis, positive thinking and imaging, home-budget management and relaxation techniques within a holistic (mind, body, spirit) environment (see Appendices G and H). I assist him when he teaches his classes, and have learned much in that capacity.

One of the things that Walt stresses is that people have different ways of dealing with problem situations. When faced with a problem, you can do one of three things. Option one - do something to change it. Option two - do nothing to change it. Option three - create something new and different. The choice you make determines whether or not you accomplish your goal, as well as what form the goal will eventually take.

There are people who believe in themselves and their ability to make things happen. These people are comfortable pursuing any of the three options. While they recognize what can and can't be done, they are also open to possibilities. The sky is not the limit for them. They "know" that they can accomplish what they set out to do. I call them *knowings*. Then, there are people, who doubt their own abilities. They are the nay-sayers, and complainers who say "no" to all options. They would probably not choose either option one or three. My guess is that they would feel most comfortable doing nothing about a problem situation, just because it's easier. Some would call them pessimists. I call them *no-ings*.

This seems like a good time to revisit my fantasy story about the two groups of people living on an island, with one great mountain called Olympus.

The *no-ings* lived in a city called Chaos and the *knowings* lived in a city called Caring. The only things that these groups had in common were that: (1) the majority of residents living in both cities were called "patients," because they needed to take pharmaceutical drugs requiring medical prescriptions of one kind or another, and (2) the only other people allowed to live in either city were their caregivers and their doctors/practitioners.

As a group, the *no-ings* were inherently selfish. They lacked compassion for the plight of others. That's why it was easy for them to allow the four power brokers known as *the Alliance* or *the Chaos Cohorts* to rule them. The things that motivated *the Alliance* entities were a reflection of the true nature of the *no-ings*. The *no-ings* did not understand what thinking outside of the box meant. They were not comfortable with change. They looked for ways to please members of *the Alliance* in order to gain favors. They really believed that there was nothing better than what they had. Little did they suspect that the consequence of allowing *the Alliance* to use them in this manner would be their own enslavement.

The Chaos Cohorts believed that the *no-ings* worshiped them as gods. In reality, some of the *no-ings* feared them while others admired them. Having *the Alliance* around reinforced how the *no-ings* saw themselves. Therefore, they saw nothing wrong about treating each other in the same way as they were treated by *the Alliance*. The exception to this was a segment of their population known as "veterans."

The Alliance knew about the veterans and made numerous unsuccessful attempts to destroy them. The veterans were change agents. They wanted things to be different, but could not accomplish their agenda because their numbers were too few. Their cause would eventually gain momentum following the return of the "travelling veteran" and the observations shared by him.

The Chaos Cohorts had no respect for the opinions of doctors/practitioners who were not under their direct control. The *no-ings* held similar views about these professionals. Caregivers were tolerated, but not valued for the essential role they played.

The Alliance used the "light of all lights" as a tool. Alleging that this tool possessed certain powers (which in reality it did not) was a way for *the Alliance* to maintain the status quo. This reputation kept the *no-ings* from asking too many questions, especially about why it was easier for certain segments of their population to gain access to drugs kept in the warehouse, especially the pharmaceutical drugs requiring medical prescriptions.

The Chaos Cohorts embedded their own criteria into a process called "prior authorization." Initially designed as a way to help people, the prior authorization process became a force of evil when *the Chaos Cohorts* used it as an instrument of discrimination. They created and used their own criteria based upon whatever they wanted it to be. Those who were denied approval suffered horribly before they died.

The residents living in the city of Chaos faced adversity. At some point, they all realized the truth of their situation. Some chose to leave the city and move to Caring. Some chose to remain in Chaos and create change from within their homeland. Both groups were successful, even though their dreams were not realized in the same way.

Once they accepted the truth about their dilemma, the way in which the residents of Chaos responded allowed them to move to a higher level and bears testament to three things. The first was that knowledge is power, because it provided the strength to counter false beliefs and the motivation to consider new possibilities. However, the ability to move forward in a productive and positive manner called for the understanding that this power should be treated with humility and respect. The second was the importance of developing a good philosophy of life that could be called upon to guide them in the right direction so that they would not lose their way. The third was making a commitment to never again settle for less from life than they truly deserved.

The residents living in Caring were called *knowings*. They were quite different from those who lived in Chaos. The *knowings* were by nature a benevolent people. They also had a prior authorization process; but, used it as it was originally intended - for the betterment of their people. This made their city prosperous, and a wonderful place to live.

As they were more evolved, the citizens of Caring approached problems logically, rather than with pure emotion or hidden agendas. They rejoiced in their ability to problem solve and think strategically, as well as their freedom to do something positive with what they discovered. They were independent thinkers who took pride in asking questions and "thinking outside of the box."

No one entity, or group of entities, was designated as the ruler of Caring. Every patient had an opportunity to gain access to the drugs kept in their warehouse, both over-the-counter and pharmaceutical requiring medical prescriptions. The only requirement was that the drug had been prescribed by a patient's doctor/practitioner and was appropriate, given the condition to be treated.

Opinions of doctors/practitioners and caregivers were rarely challenged. Cases earmarked by doctors/practitioners as "medical necessity, please expedite," were given priority. Doctors/practitioners were highly respected members of the community, and their opinions were greatly valued. Caregivers were seen as angels of mercy. They were the ones charged with the day-to-day responsibilities which insured the health and wellbeing of the patients. They were admired and respected for their dedication, compassion and positive attitudes.

The *knowings* living in Caring knew about the difficulties facing the residents in Chaos. They knew about *the Alliance* and the tactics they used to redirect attention away from the truth about what they were really doing. They understood that the residents of Chaos were the architects of their own dilemma.

The interesting thing was that the residents in Caring did not fear *the Chaos Cohorts*. Being more evolved than the residents in Chaos, they understood that there were three possible options when faced with a problem- do something about it, do nothing about it, or create something new and different. The outcome would be directly related to whatever choice was made.

The residents of Caring knew that without their permission, *the Chaos Cohorts* (aka *the Alliance*) would never rule them. The *knowings* were in control of their own lives and therefore their own destinies. The true nature of the *knowings* was far different than that of *the Alliance* entities. They were certainly not motivated by the same things. *The Alliance* had nothing to hang their hats on in their city.

The citizens of Caring welcomed anyone from Chaos, as long as they were willing to give-up their pessimistic, self-defeating philosophy and adopt a new mindset, especially concerning how the prior authorization process could be used to help everyone thrive. Being as evolved as they were, in a way the *knowings* were "seers." They knew that rejecting the control of *the Alliance* meant that the *no-ings* were now free to evolve to a higher level, if they chose to do so. They firmly believed that this would happen, given support and encouragement. However, the *knowings* respected both groups - those who chose to relocate, as well as those who decided to remain in Chaos and create change from within. They credited both groups as being successful, even though the process by which their dreams were going to be realized would differ.

In my fantasy story, the solution to the problem came quickly. The "light of all lights" grew dimmer as residents of Chaos left the city. Those residents who decided to remain did so with the understanding that they were going to work together to create something new and different without leaving their homeland. They were not going to continue to let others define what they needed or could have, especially when done unfairly. They were tired of being victimized.

They deserved better. It might take time, but they were going to save themselves. They were becoming *know-ings*!

Sadly, this resolution might not happen as quickly (or as neatly) in the real world in which we live. Let's look at the situation facing those of us living in the United States today. *The Alliance,* otherwise known as *the Chaos Cohorts*, is not a fantasy. These entities really exist. They exert tremendous power and authority and touch the lives of each of us in one way or another on a daily basis.

Allowing *the Chaos Cohorts* to exert this kind of authority and control has resulted in dire consequences for many, especially patients in need of legitimate access to pharmaceutical drugs requiring medical prescriptions. The question becomes: What can we do to help ourselves and those we care for, despite their efforts to use the prior authorization process in a way that creates barriers to the legitimate access of pharmaceutical drugs requiring medical prescriptions? Perhaps the best approach to solving this question lies in a consideration of the following words:

"God grant me the serenity to accept
The things I cannot change!
Courage to change the things I can,
And Knowledge, Wisdom, Understanding,
And Inner- Vision,
To know the difference"! [9]

Most of you might recognize this as *the Serenity Prayer* (original version modified by Walt in his book, *Poetry to Inspire Healing: Let Your Light Shine! 2014*), one of the acknowledged guides to follow when it comes to making decisions. The original version of this poem speaks to the need for <u>serenity</u>, <u>courage</u>, and <u>wisdom</u> when understanding the difference between what can and can't be changed.

These three tools are pretty much self-explanatory. I sincerely doubt that anyone could discount their importance. As caregivers, we already have too many things to do. It makes no sense to use what remains of our precious energy and time worrying about things which we cannot change. Together with these three tools, I would suggest that the key to overcoming barriers encountered during the prior authorization process, specifically those denying access to pharmaceutical drugs requiring medical prescriptions, lies in understanding and applying the three additional requirements added by Walt: <u>knowledge, understanding,</u> and <u>inner- vision</u>.

<u>Knowledge</u>. The *knowings* living in the city of Caring knew that knowledge is power. They realized that the reason why *the Alliance* could control the patients living in Chaos was because the patients gave them the power to do so. Giving up their power resulted in them loosing the ability to see that they had a problem, grasp the severity of their problem, or even know that there were options which might have bettered their situation.

<u>Understanding</u>. I mentioned in a previous chapter that a caregiver must become knowledgeable about topics related to the medical condition of the one he/she cares for. There must be ways to identify the relevant questions which need to be asked, and sort through all of the information that is out there. Developing the ability to think logically and critically are essential skills for any caregiver to master.

<u>Inner- Vision</u>. Consider the air that we breathe. It can't be seen, touched, tasted, smelled, or felt. Yet, it is all around us. We trust that it is there. We accept its presence, because without it we know that we couldn't survive in this environment for long. This is an example of how we can use the tools of imagination, intuition, inner vision, and logical and critical thinking, when solving problems. Each time we use these tools when making decisions and experience success, we gain confidence that we followed the right course of action and

courage to use them again, when needed. As it relates to the topic of this book, this is <u>key</u> to building the confidence needed to <u>know</u> that it is possible to find ways to overcome barriers preventing legal access to appropriate pharmaceutical drugs requiring medical prescriptions. This is the way to win the battle that will eventually win this war.

<u>Imagination</u> can be used to build an image (or images) of how we want ourselves to be or goals that we want to accomplish. Confirmation that we are on the right track (or wrong track) comes from <u>intuition</u>, that inner, gut level feeling. <u>Inner vision</u> is insight, and pulls it all together into one neat package.

Remember that choices made will determine whether or not goals are accomplished. With this as a foundation, Walt and I took our first step. We decided to create a plan to help us get to where we needed to go.

CHAPTER 37
Fail to Plan, Plan to Fail

Back in 1949, Walt was stationed at the headquarters of the United States Army in Europe, Heidelberg, Germany. He was assigned there as a military intelligence administrative assistant. Working in administration provided many opportunities to observe high ranking officers during the course of their workdays. Walt especially remembers times when he would hear them speak about how they approached problem situations. It was their job to come up with game plans to force change.

One critical factor seemed to surface time and time again. That factor was the importance of planning strategically. These officers knew what their current situation was. They also knew the desired outcome. They could not afford to get caught-up in distractions. Their job was to answer the following question: What was the best thing to do in order to reach the desired goal, given everything that could be done? Sounds familiar.

There was no doubt as to the severity of the situation facing us. The more we discovered, the more it seemed that our task was monumental. How in the world would we fight foes of this nature? People with more resources and connections gave it their best shot and failed. For the two of us to try would almost be like David fighting Goliath. On the other hand, I seem to recall that David was a change agent. He defeated Goliath, because God was in his corner. After all that we had been through, I knew that God was on our side. Otherwise how could we have gotten to this point?

I considered all that we had gone through – the stress, the disappointments, the inconveniences, the delays. It was then that I realized that everything had been for a reason. God had not given us more than we could handle to discourage us. He/she had been trying to reassure us that doing our best was to be the proof that we were winners, even though the final result might not be exactly what we envisioned. We certainly could "talk the talk." Could we also "walk the walk?"

It was at that point that Walt and I made the decision to move into the city of Caring. This decision involved risks. As happened with his doctor/practitioner (nephrologist), we had to prepare for possible retaliation and persecution. This was something that we were willing to deal with, if and when the time came.

Having made this decision, we began to develop our plan. This plan would be used to guide us from this point on in what we had to do and where we wanted to go. We needed options and we needed them quickly. Despite the efforts of *the Chaos Cohorts*, what was the best way to gain access to the life saving pharmaceutical drug requiring a medical prescription that Walt so desperately needed?

CHAPTER 38
Know the Current Situation

Walt and I believe in the wisdom of understanding where you have been (or are) in order to know where you are going. We wanted to learn from mistakes so that they would not be repeated. With this in mind, we agreed that the first step in our plan would be to review what we had discovered so far.

(1) *The Chaos Cohorts* (aka *the Alliance*) are four powerful entities which really exist: biopharmaceutical companies, health insurance companies, distributors (pharmacy benefit management companies (PBM's) and wholesale distribution companies), and the federal government.

(2) All of the branches of *the Chaos Cohorts* share one common goal – to satisfy their need for power, control, and profit. Each wants to make a dollar at our expense. They will go to any extent to accomplish this, and even turn on each other in the name of increasing profit motives.

(3) *The Chaos Cohorts* misuse a process (prior authorization), initially designed for good, by turning it into a force of evil. They use limited criteria of their own design to dictate who will gain access to life-saving pharmaceutical drugs requiring medical prescriptions. This is a form of discrimination which, in effect, complicates existing conditions and sentences some patients to pain, suffering, and eventual death.

(4) Health insurance companies partner with distributors- wholesale distribution companies and pharmacy benefit management companies (PBM's). PBM's act as middle-men between biopharmaceutical companies and health insurance companies, and also perform administrative duties. When PBM's,

"rubber stamp" recommendations made by health insurance companies, which compromise the health and well being of patients to satisfy their own agendas, their true natures are exposed as branches of *the Chaos Cohorts.*

(5) Wholesale distribution companies and pharmacy benefit management companies (PBM's) hire pharmaceutical sales representatives to market their products to doctors/practitioners and pharmacies.

(6) *The Chaos Cohorts* create provocative and entertaining distractions (for example, sensational news items overflowing with drama) so that they can hide their true agenda (creating laws and regulations geared toward serving their own purposes) from public view.

(7) The media keeps these distractions in front of the public in the form of news items. Time devoted to viewing these items could be better spent raising thoughts to higher levels, which is where they need to be in order to see beyond the deception. Getting to a higher level allows people to start asking questions which might challenge what *the Chaos Cohorts* are actually doing. This is something that they want to avoid at all costs. They don't want things to turn around so that satisfying the needs of patients becomes the focus of this countries love.

(8) Our government (a branch of *the Chaos Cohorts*) has a long and shameful track record when it comes to using tactics such as deceit, deception, confusion, and apathy to accomplish self-serving goals. These "bait and switch" tactics were used with <u>veterans</u> as a group (for example, WWII) when promises were made to repay "honor, service and sacrifice" with *free medical healthcare*. They used them with <u>African American veterans</u>, historically victims of racism, discrimination and insensitivity, who were seeking greater access to equity in health care, educational and financial options. They used them with <u>patients</u> (for example, those having kidney disease

and on hemodialysis), by advertising and marketing at least one life-saving prescription medication without making it clear that there would be some who would qualify for it, some who would not qualify for it, and what was needed to qualify for it in the first place. With this analysis as a foundation, Walt and I were now ready to go on to the next step in our plan.

CHAPTER 39
Count Your Blessings

What comes to mind when I mention the word, asset? If you are like most people, you probably view an asset as something that has value that can be used to make a profit with or exchanged for a service. Money, jewelry, houses, and cars are examples of assets. An asset can also represent characteristics that you have in your favor. Being attentive, considerate, dependable and kind are assets hopefully seen in a person claiming to be a caregiver.

Identifying our assets (as a team and individually) was the <u>second</u> step in our plan to determine the best way to gain access to the life saving pharmaceutical drug requiring a medical prescription Walt needed. With this in mind, I sat down and began to make a list of what we had going for us in our favor. The points which follow were a few of these things.

(1) Both Walt and I are personally committed to the same goal of helping him gain access to the pharmaceutical drug needed to control his bad LDL cholesterol.

(2) Walt has a background in teaching positive thinking and imaging. This information has helped both of us remain positive and optimistic.

(3) I have a basic familiarity with computer technology and organizational skills. That has certainly proven useful for record keeping and chronicling events.

(4) One consequence of assuming the responsibility of being Walt's caregiver is that I have developed a "thick-skin" in order to deal with most problems. I have a tendency to quickly respond with a "come-back at you attitude" when faced with set-backs. I might get knocked down, but I'm never knocked-out!

(5) I ask a lot of questions.
(6) My memory and listening skills are reasonable, which lets me retain a lot of information for future investigation.
(7) We have a team of highly trained health care professionals willing to help us by dedicating time, energy and information.
(8) Divine intervention.

Chapter 40
The Shortest Distance Between Two Points

Following a determination of what we knew and our assets, the <u>third</u> step in our plan involved looking at what had been done and by whom. Even though attempted, none of these maneuvers had been successful in helping us accomplish our goal. However, doing this analysis prepared us for the <u>final</u> step, which was to generate practical options to address our problem.

(1) Walt's doctor/practitioner (nephrologist) who initiated the prior authorization process had completed and submitted the paperwork (initial request and subsequent appeal) required by the health insurance company (one branch of *the Chaos Cohorts*). This paperwork included data stating that the pharmaceutical drug was a "medical necessity" needed to control his bad LDL cholesterol.

(2) I collected additional data (lipid panel results) tracking Walt's response to free samples of the pharmaceutical drug requiring a medical prescription supplied by his doctors/practitioners and submitted a summary to Walt's nephrologist, who then submitted this information to the health insurance company.

(3) Several cardiologists had been visited in an attempt to find one with enough professional integrity to certify in writing that Walt met the criteria for a diagnosis of ASCVD (Atherosclerotic Cardiovascular Disease). Having this disease was one of three conditions specified as a prerequisite by the health insurance company for obtaining prior authorization approval of the drug needed to control his bad LDL cholesterol.

(4) We scheduled and paid money out-of-pocket for a preventive health screening for Walt, which confirmed the presence of atherosclerotic cardiovascular disease (ASCVD).
(5) Several trips had been made to doctors/practitioners offices in order to obtain free samples of the prescription medication needed to control Walt's bad LDL cholesterol.
(6) Walt and I assumed the responsibility of making sure that his doctor/practitioner (nephrologist) received copies (in a timely manner) of any correspondence sent to us by the health insurance company or the PBM (pharmacy benefit management company).
(7) Walt and I notified several newspapers and magazines, hoping to generate interest in our situation. The only response received was from one on-line newspaper.

CHAPTER 41
Will the Cavalry Come to Our Rescue?

Given all that had been tried and failed, thinking outside of the box and strategic planning were the only things left in our war chest. Having to go to an unfamiliar level often tests what you are really made of, especially if going there calls for you to deal with activities which are necessary but not within your everyday comfort zone.

Walt's doctor/practitioner (nephrologist) followed all of the steps mandated by the prior authorization process utilized by the health insurance company. He completed and submitted all of the required paperwork and invested more than the average amount of time and energy as the case had gone to appeal. Walt and I had assumed responsibilities in excess of those expected of patients and their caregivers. Nothing had worked to this point. We were still dependent upon free samples of the prescription medication Walt needed in order to control his bad LDL cholesterol.

At this point we were becoming really desperate. We knew that life would be difficult if Walt had to go on depending upon these free samples. It was then that I decided to "up the ante." We were taking a risk, and it was late in the game, but a different approach was required.

Walt and I made no claim to be counted among the rich and famous segment of society. We were in no position to make substantial contributions in order to buy any kind of political assistance. However, we were constituents, and as such, claimed the power that accompanied voting privileges. Whether or not this would result in attention being paid to us was another question.

I'll admit that I was having a moment of weakness. Like the residents of the fantasy city of Chaos, maybe we should just fall in line and offer special gifts of money to members of *the Chaos Cohorts* as a way of trying to get what we wanted. After all, there is a thin line between fantasy and reality. Given everything that had happened, there was more than enough evidence to confirm that we were indeed living in the land of the *no-ings*. I had no idea as to what might happen. In an unexpected move, I made telephone calls to two agents of the federal government (a branch of *the Chaos Cohorts*).

Senators and Congressman are part of the federal government. These are elected officials. While each state has two Senators, the number of Congressman may vary depending upon the population of the state. They have been known to respond to requests for assistance made by people living in their districts, to include problems involving federal agencies. Since everything else had failed, I decided that it was worth a try.

I made telephone calls to the offices of both the Senator and Representative for our district. Their staff persons asked a number of background questions and told me that they would forward our information to the appropriate party.

Following that conversation, we received a call-back from the office of our Congressman. The staff person with whom we spoke seemed interested in our problem. He requested that we send them background information and supporting documents. We were given a case number. We also had to sign a release of information form (generated by the office of the Congressman which included his official U.S. House of Representative seal), giving our consent for his office to represent and obtain information on our behalf.

I'll have to give credit to our Congressman, who contacted the health insurance company several times. Considering everything else that had been attempted, contacting him was the one tactic which seemed to raise a few eyebrows when it came to getting a response from the health insurance company and pharmacy benefit manager (PBM).

Then, something happened that once and for all confirmed that the tiger was not going to change its stripes. Remember that one of Walt's insurance plans is through the military. Evidently our case caught the attention of someone in a power position. The big guns took notice and they came out firing!

Approximately five months after the initial inquiry by our Congressman, we received (for the first time) a letter from the top agency responsible for administering the health insurance plan, stating that another authorization form (to disclose medical or dental information) was needed in order for their office to speak with the Congressman representing us (see Appendix T). The authorization form generated by the Congressman's office wasn't good enough – the agency responsible for administering the health insurance plan wanted to use their own form. Ironically, factions of the federal government were fighting each other.

On top of everything else, Walt and I were now victims of the red tape of the bureaucracy of *the Chaos Cohorts*.

It has now been almost one year since we have heard anything from either the health insurance company or the Congressman. My fear is that our problem has been lost in a war of their egos. Then, my own words come back to haunt me: "When all else fails, keep it light, because the dark side is just too heavy." I guess that only time will tell.

CHAPTER 42
If I Woulda- Shoulda- Coulda Club

As a child, I enjoyed putting puzzles together. Of course, knowing what the final picture would look like in advance made working with more complex designs less frustrating. Being able to find meaning in the things that life presents in some respects is like working with puzzles. It's easier to arrive at solutions if you initially know what you are working with. There is truth in the saying that hindsight is 20/20.

Are there times when it would be wise for patients (and their caregivers) to know more (or at least as much) about their medical conditions than their doctors/practitioners do before agreeing to take a drug or undergo a certain procedure? Based upon everything that I discovered, the answer to this question is a resounding, yes.

If only I could turn back time. I wonder what kept me from seeing this basic truth when we started our journey. Maybe I believed that patients/caregivers should be free to be patients/caregivers and not medical experts. After all, I already had too much on my plate to begin with. Maybe I really wanted our problem to be taken care of by someone else, just like the doctor/practitioner of my childhood days did for his patients. Maybe I trusted that Walt's doctor/practitioner (nephrologist) would actually have the power to accomplish a miracle. He had never been challenged about anything that he prescribed for Walt prior to this incident. Maybe like the participants in the Tuskegee Experiment and the veterans in 1948, I just trusted everyone to do the right thing.

Today, our very survival as patients and caregivers of those we love depends upon being ever-vigilant about the status of health care in this country. There was a time when my only responsibility as a caregiver was to help the one I cared for with difficult tasks. As a patient, my doctors/practitioners used to take care of everything related to any illness that I had. I did not have to worry about what medication to take, whether or not it was correct, or paperwork involved in qualifying for it. My confidence that the right decisions were being made on my behalf allowed me to concentrate on one thing – getting well.

We now live in a very different world. It's obvious that our roles as patients and caregivers have been redefined, and not by us. In order to survive in today's world, patients and caregivers must assume responsibilities never dreamed of by those in the past. If I could go back in time armed with the knowledge that I have today, there are definitely some things that I would do differently as far as helping Walt gain access to the medication prescribed by the one doctor/practitioner who knows him the best, his nephrologist.

Walt's doctor/practitioner (nephrologist) gave him samples of a brand name prescription medication. Walt tried the free samples and found that this prescription medication lived up to its reputation. Based upon what I now know, as soon as the pharmacist informed us that he was unable to fill the prescription, I would have begun a thorough investigation of this drug to include what was necessary to obtain it. In this case, my investigation would have revealed a need for prior authorization. I would have learned more about the prior authorization process, especially which doctors/practitioners were sanctioned by the health insurance company to prescribe this prescription medication. We would have "shopped around" and compiled a list of cardiologists willing to certify in writing that Walt had one of the recognized medical conditions (ASCVD) and therefore qualified for the needed medication. Those having unsuccessful track records obtaining this medication for patients would be excluded from our list. Those having successful track records would be contacted and interviewed. A final choice would be made by us based upon that interview. We would have reached out to our Congressman much earlier in the game and shared information about what we were trying to accomplish. This would be done in anticipation of possibly needing his assistance. I am not going to beat up on myself too much, given all that has happened, After all, life is full of lessons to be learned and there will always be another battle to fight, and war to win.

CHAPTER 43:
Caregiver Reflections

When everything seems to suggest failure, I remember that it's not where you start but where you <u>end</u> that's important. I made two observations when I began writing this book. The first was that there was a possibility that I might not like what I discovered. The second was that even in the face of disappointment, I still had a responsibility to do something worthwhile and positive with what was discovered.

I continue to believe that knowledge is power, and that this power should be treated with respect and humility. Walt and I remain confident that some day we will realize our dream of obtaining a legitimate prescription for the only pharmaceutical option available to control his bad LDL cholesterol. No one can say that we did not give it all that we had to give. No one can say that others who came to our assistance failed to do likewise.

The preponderance of the evidence confirms that the Unites States and the fantasy city of Chaos are one in the same. This reality must be faced. We have been and are living in the land of the *no-ings*. *The Chaos Cohorts* (aka *the Alliance*) exists. We have allowed ourselves to become their victims. *The Alliance* formed by these entities assumes a level of authority and power which, if unchecked, has control of our very existence in a way that was never imagined.

This didn't happen over- night. It has been going on for a very, very long time. The plight of the veterans in 1948 and the fate of the participants in the Tuskegee Study are just a few examples in a long list of appalling events.

CHAPTER 44
The Way is Clear

While this may not be the right time to put *the Chaos Cohorts* out of business, there are some things that can be done to make their existence uncomfortable. Addressing issues inherent within the prior authorization process which create barriers to the legitimate access of prescription medication is a good place to start.

Walt and I found that contacting our Congressman was the most effective tactic when it came to getting anything like a "worried" response from the health insurance company and pharmacy benefit management company (PBM). Having supportive documentation to share with that Representative proved critical.

Perhaps you, or someone you are caring for, have also been abused by this process. If so, my challenge to every patient and caregiver reading this book is that you contact your state Representative (Congressman or Senator) and share your concerns about how this process is being implemented. That person might be able to at least make inquiries on your behalf, and even agree to take up your cause, especially if it aligns with one of their own priorities. If they don't support you, then vote for someone else who will.

I invite you to encourage your Representative to sponsor legislation which supports reframing the prior authorization process. If you are in agreement with me that things need to change, then let your Representative know how unfair the current process is. Feel free to refer to the data and arguments presented in this book, if need be.

In my opinion, there is a pronounced discrepancy between the initial intent of the prior authorization process and how it is being used by those in power (for example, health insurance companies and pharmacy benefit management companies). They are denying access to pharmaceutical drugs requiring medical prescriptions which unjustly discriminates against so many people who have a legitimate need for this intervention.

In my opinion, several <u>key</u> components of the prior authorization process (as currently written) need to be reframed as follows.

<u>Criteria</u>. Access to any pharmaceutical drug requiring a medical prescription (for example, one advertised as being able to control bad LDL levels) should not be denied for any reason, as long as the referral is legitimate and the patient can benefit from it.

<u>Specialists</u>. The doctor/practitioner prescribing a pharmaceutical drug requiring a medical prescription (for example, one advertised as lowering bad LDL cholesterol levels) should not be excluded from the decision making process, solely on the basis of his/her specialty area. If a doctor/practitioner prescribes a medication for any use that the medication was intended to perform, and that doctor/practitioner is assuming a primary role in the care of a patient for whom the medication is being prescribed (for example, nephrologist for a patient on hemodialysis), then the recommendation of that doctor/practitioner should be regarded as sufficient by any agency having the power to grant access to that medication. Access to the medication should not be denied just because the doctor/practitioner does not practice in a specialty area as specified by a health insurance company or a pharmacy benefit manager.

<u>Prerequisites</u>. A patient should not be denied access to a pharmaceutical drug requiring a medical prescription (for example, one advertised as lowering bad LDL cholesterol levels) because he/she refuses to start treatment on a less expensive or weaker form of another drug in order to prove to a health insurance company or pharmacy benefit management company that those drugs don't work. Patient safety and well-being should supersede profit motive.

<u>Medical Necessity</u>. A decision that a pharmaceutical drug requiring a medical prescription (for example, one advertised as lowering bad LDL cholesterol levels) is "a medical necessity," when made by a doctor/practitioner assuming a primary role in the care of a patient for whom the drug is being prescribed (for example, nephrologist for a patient on hemodialysis), should be regarded as sufficient by any agency (for example, health insurance company or pharmacy benefit management company) having the power to grant access to that drug.

I think that the *knowings* living in the fantasy city of Caring were onto something beautiful. If we truly want to turn this country into one where people thrive, then let us start with equity of health care. We need to stop pledging allegiance to *the Chaos Cohorts* and start pledging allegiance to <u>improving the quality of health care for all of our citizens, regardless of racial or ethnic status, age, gender, challenge or ability to pay</u>. The "powers that be" in this country need to stop making "hollow" promises which only benefit a few and start making real commitments to actually do what will help everyone.

CHAPTER 45
Conclusion

Short of divine intervention, I feel less positive about an outcome other than the present one regarding the promise of *free medical health care for life* made by this government in 1948 to so many young military enlistees like Walt.

But, who knows what the future will bring. Life is full of possibilities. It may be that we will see the resolution of Walt's dilemma, but not in the way in which we envisioned it. It is our hope that sharing his story ignites the spark which creates a flame in others that will bring our dream to fruition. Maybe reading stories like ours will serve as a wake-up call for anyone who continues to minimize or deny how much the desire for profit influences the quality of care that patients receive from the health care industry in this country.

It is a given that people will resort to any means necessary to relieve their pain and suffering. I believe that nothing should be put in the way of a patient having access to any medical remedy that is legitimate, and that will improve quality of life and alleviate pain and suffering. The power players in this country obviously have their own agenda(s). As a caregiver, I propose that we start developing agenda(s) which will work for us and for those we love and care for. Can I get an "amen" from the congregation?

EPILOGUE

Don't worry about Walt. He is the love of my life. We have a lovely home in a great community and all of the material things that we could ever want or wish for. We have good people of all ages around us, many of whom are children and young people who call Walt, "Dad." Walt's nephrologist tells us that, given his great support system (that would be me) he should live well past the age of 100. In the meantime, his immediate future is secure. Thank God for those free samples! Still, we are committed to doing whatever we can to help patients and their caregivers overcome barriers encountered during the prior authorization process when attempting to obtain legitimate access to pharmaceutical drugs requiring medical prescriptions.

Our journey has just begun. Walt and I know that we have a long way to go and that there will be difficult decisions to make. As always, we will figure things out together. One thing is for sure. We will no longer be content to live in the city of Chaos. From now on, we **will** hang our hats in the city of Caring. The question is: Where will you hang yours? Patient or profit…. Where is the love?

If you wish to contact me, please do so at:
skitldu@gmail.com.

REFERENCES

1. "Multiracial Americans." (last edited 4 February 2018). *Wikipedia The Free Encyclopedia.* Retrieved 26 December 2017 from https://en.wikipedia.org/wiki/Multiracial_Americans.

2. "Douglas MacArthur." (last edited 21 December 2017). *Wikipedia The Free Encyclopedia.* Retrieved 21 December 2017 from https://en.wikipedia.org/wiki/Douglas_MacArthur.

3. Hammond, Walter B.(D.D.). (2014). *Poetry To Inspire Healing: Let Your Light Shine!* Las Vegas, NV: Hammond, Walter B. (D.D.).

4. "Walter Bernard Hammond, D.D." (Fall Quarter Edition 2014:43). Melville, NY: *Industry Experts Magazine.*

5. "Food and Drug Administration." (last edited on 18 January 2018) *Wikipedia The Free Encyclopedia.* Retrieved 27 November 2017 from https://en.wikipedia.org/wiki/Food_and_Drug_Administration.

6. "Food and Drug Administration." (last edited on 26 October 2017). *Wikipedia The Free Encyclopedia.* Retrieved 26 October 2017 from https://en.wikipedia.org/wiki/Food_and_Drug_Administration.

7. "Pharmacists Manual - Section IX-XIV." (Revised 2010). *US Department of Justice - Drug Enforcement Administration.* Retrieved 15 November 2017 from https://www.deadiversion.usdoj.gov/pubs/manuals/

pharm2/pharm_content.htm.

8. Hammond, Walter B.(D.D.). (2014). *Poetry To Inspire Healing: Let Your Light Shine!* Las Vegas, NV: Hammond, Walter B. (D.D.).

APPENDICES

A. Dr. Walter B. Hammond and Dr. Adah F. Kennon in Maui, Hawaii (before kidney disease)
B. Edith Randall Hayes (Walt's Mother)
C. Winston Perselle Hammond (Walt's Father)
D. Walt, High School Graduate
E. Walt, First Sergeant at 23-years of age
F. Walt Returns Stateside (with Mother, Edith)
G. Dr. Walter Bernard Hammond, Owner and Teacher, Development of Relaxation Powers
H. Dr. Walter B. Hammond, Hypnosis Certificate
I. Dr. Walter B. Hammond, Jefferson Award Winner
J. Dr. Walter B. Hammond, Jefferson Award Certificate
K. Dr. Walter B. Hammond, Author
L. Dr. Walter B. Hammond, Bowling (Before Kidney Disease)
M. Dr. Walter B. Hammond and Dr. Adah F. Kennon, Wedding, 1990
N. Dr. Walter B. Hammond Birthday Party at Dialysis Center (with Dr. Adah F. Kennon), 2017
O. First Medical Necessity Letter, dated February 8, 2017
P. Reconsideration of Denial Letter from Department of Defense, dated March 8, 2017 (cc to Dr. Walter B. Hammond)
Q. Follow-up Letter to Telephone Conversation Upholding Denial, dated June 7, 2017 to Dr. Walter B. Hammond
R. Second Medical Necessity Letter, dated June 9, 2017
S. Copy of letter to Nephrologist Denying Appeal Reconsideration, dated July 11, 2017
T. Response to Representative Letter from Department of Defense Requesting Additional Release Form sent to Dr. Walter B. Hammond, dated August 15, 2017

Appendix A

Dr. Walter B. Hammond and Dr. Adah F. Kennon in Maui, Hawaii (before kidney disease)

Appendix B

Edith Randall Hayes Hammond (Walt's mother)

Appendix C

Winston Perselle Hammond (Walt's father)

Appendix D

Walt, High School Graduate

Appendix E

Walt, First Sergeant at 23 – years of age

Appendix F

Walt Returns Stateside (with mother, Edith)

Appendix G

Dr. Walter Bernard Hammond, owner and teacher, Development of Relaxation Powers

Appendix H

Dr. Walter B. Hammond, Hypnosis Certificate

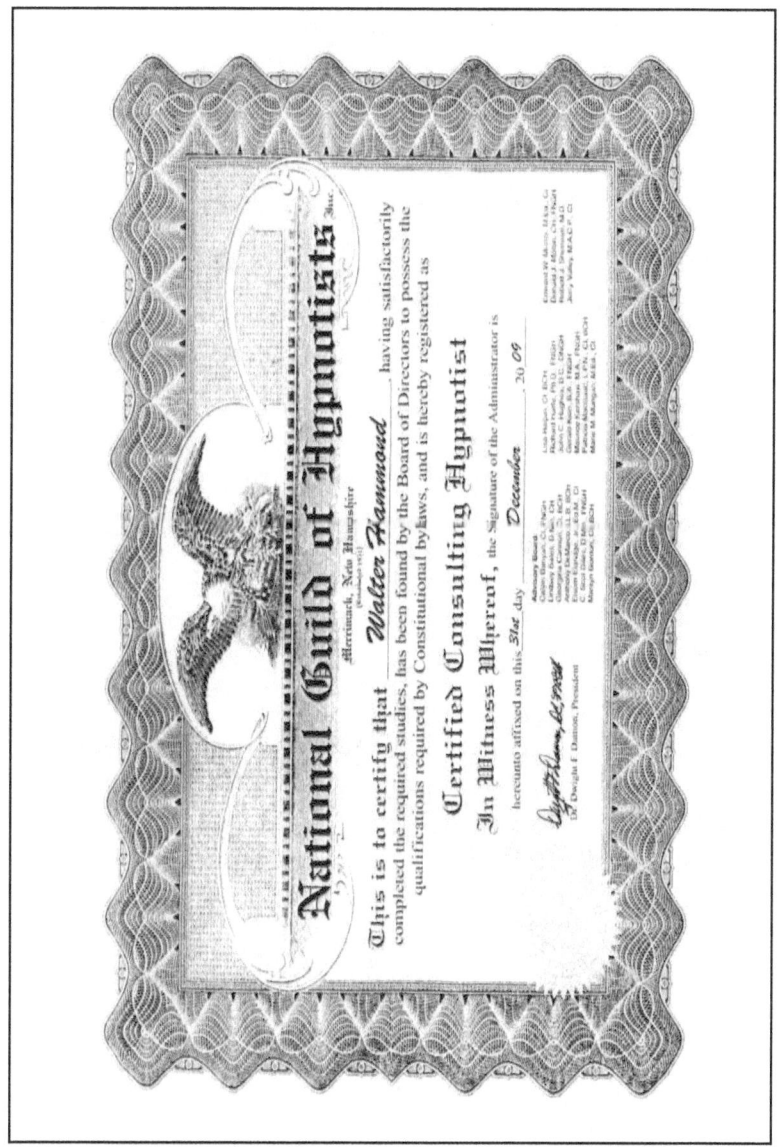

Appendix I
Dr. Walter B. Hammond, Jefferson Award Winner

Appendix J

Dr. Walter B. Hammond, Jefferson Award Certificate

Appendix K

Dr. Walter B. Hammond, Author
(Available, Amazon.com)

Appendix L

Dr. Walter B. Hammond, Bowling (Before Kidney Disease)

Appendix M

Dr. Walter B. Hammond and Dr. Adah F. Kennon, Wedding, 1990

Appendix N

Dr. Walter B. Hammond Birthday Party at Dialysis Center
(with Dr. Adah F. Kennon), 2017

Appendix O

First Medical Necessity Letter, dated February 8, 2017

03-14-'17 13:55 FROM-   T-137 P0001/0008 F-

Appendix N

ATTN: Appeals
Please expidite

To Whom It May Concern: Attn ▮▮▮▮ Case # 3741792, ▮▮▮▮

I am writing on behalf of my patient, (**Walter Hammond D.OB 6/2/1930**) to document the medical necessity of ▮▮▮▮ for the treatment of (E 78.00 Pure Hypocholesteremia, ASCVD I 25.10).

Patient's History and Diagnosis: (History of elevated cholesterol DX Pure hypercholesterolemia and ASCVD patient unable to tolerate statins due to contraindications muscle pain)

Treatment Rationale: (Patient has tried and failed other lower lipid lowering agents ▮▮▮▮ , the use of ▮▮▮▮ will help to reduce patients high cholesterol .)

Duration: (12 months ▮▮▮▮ 11 refills)

Summary: In summary (▮▮▮▮ is medically necessary for this patient's medical condition. Please contact me if any additional information is required to ensure the prompt approval of ▮▮▮▮ .

Sincerely, Dr. ▮▮▮▮   2-08-17

Appendix P

Reconsideration of Denial Letter from Department of Defense, dated March 8, 2017 (cc to Dr. Walter B. Hammond) – Page 1

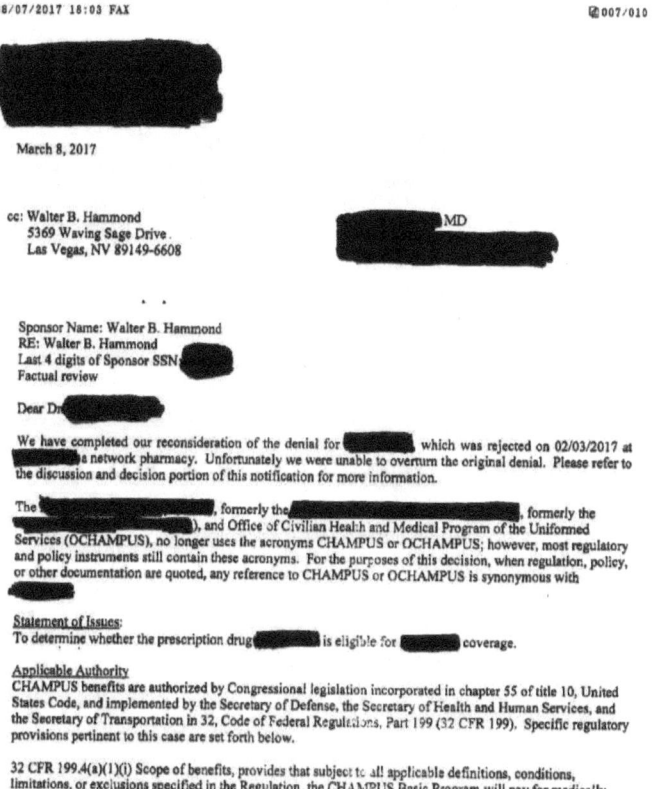

08/07/2017 18:03 FAX ⌀007/010

March 8, 2017

cc: Walter B. Hammond
5369 Waving Sage Drive
Las Vegas, NV 89149-6608

MD

Sponsor Name: Walter B. Hammond
RE: Walter B. Hammond
Last 4 digits of Sponsor SSN:
Factual review

Dear Dr

We have completed our reconsideration of the denial for ▮▮▮▮ which was rejected on 02/03/2017 at ▮▮▮▮ a network pharmacy. Unfortunately we were unable to overturn the original denial. Please refer to the discussion and decision portion of this notification for more information.

The ▮▮▮▮, formerly the ▮▮▮▮, formerly the ▮▮▮▮), and Office of Civilian Health and Medical Program of the Uniformed Services (OCHAMPUS), no longer uses the acronyms CHAMPUS or OCHAMPUS; however, most regulatory and policy instruments still contain these acronyms. For the purposes of this decision, when regulation, policy, or other documentation are quoted, any reference to CHAMPUS or OCHAMPUS is synonymous with ▮▮▮▮.

Statement of Issues:
To determine whether the prescription drug ▮▮▮▮ is eligible for ▮▮▮▮ coverage.

Applicable Authority
CHAMPUS benefits are authorized by Congressional legislation incorporated in chapter 55 of title 10, United States Code, and implemented by the Secretary of Defense, the Secretary of Health and Human Services, and the Secretary of Transportation in 32, Code of Federal Regulations, Part 199 (32 CFR 199). Specific regulatory provisions pertinent to this case are set forth below.

32 CFR 199.4(a)(1)(i) Scope of benefits, provides that subject to all applicable definitions, conditions, limitations, or exclusions specified in the Regulation, the CHAMPUS Basic Program will pay for medically necessary services and supplies required in the diagnosis and treatment of illness or injury, including maternity care and well-baby care.

32 CFR 199.2(b) defines appropriate medical care in pertinent part as that medical care where the services performed in connection with the diagnosis or treatment of disease or injury, pregnancy, mental disorder, or well-baby care are in keeping with the generally accepted norms for medical practice in the United States and

Letter Generated: 03/08/17 2:01 PM

where the authorized individual professional provider rendering the medical care is qualified to perform such medical services by reason of his or her training and education and is licensed or certified by the state where the service is rendered or appropriate national organization or otherwise meets CHAMPUS standards. The definition also specifies that the medical environment in which the medical services are performed is the least expensive level of care and adequate to provide the required medical care regardless of whether the level of care is covered by CHAMPUS.

32 CFR 199.2(b) defines medically or psychologically necessary in pertinent part as the frequency, extent, and types of medical services or supplies which represent appropriate medical care and that are generally accepted by qualified professionals to be reasonable and adequate for the diagnosis and treatment of illness, injury, pregnancy, and mental disorders or that are reasonable and adequate for well-baby care.

32 CFR 199.4(a)(5) Right to information. As a condition precedent to the provision of benefits, OCHAMPUS or its OCHAMPUS [contractors]... shall be entitled to receive information from a physician or hospital or other person, institution, or organization (including a local, state, or U.S. Government agency) providing services or supplies to the beneficiary for which claims or requests for approval of benefits are submitted. Such information and records may relate to the attendance, testing, monitoring, or examination or diagnosis of, or treatment rendered, or services and supplies furnished to a beneficiary, and shall be necessary for the accurate and efficient administration of CHAMPUS benefits. Before a determination will be made on a request for preauthorization or claim of benefits, a beneficiary or sponsor must provide particular additional information relevant to the requested determination, when necessary, which information will, subject to certain specific exclusions, be held confidential by the recipient.

32 CFR 199.4(g)(63) Noncovered condition, unauthorized provider. All services and supplies (including inpatient institutional costs) related to a noncovered condition or treatment, or provided by an unauthorized provider are specifically excluded from the Basic Program.

32 CFR 199.4(g)(74) Exclusions and limitations. In addition to any definitions, requirements, conditions, or limitations enumerated and described in other sections of this part, the following specifically are excluded from the Basic Program: (1) Not medically or psychologically necessary. Services and supplies that are not medically or psychologically necessary for the diagnosis or treatment of a covered illness (including mental disorder) or injury, for the diagnosis and treatment of pregnancy or well-baby care.

32 CFR 199.4(g) Exclusions and limitations. Note: The fact that a physician may prescribe, order, recommend, or approve a service or supply does not, of itself, make it medically necessary or make the charge an allowable expense, even though it is not listed specifically as an exclusion.

32 CFR 199.4(a)(13) specifies that the Director, OCHAMPUS, shall issue policies, procedures, instructions, guidelines, standards and/or criteria to implement 32 CFR 199...

32 CFR 199.10 (a)(9) Appeal decision. An appeal decision at any level may address all pertinent issues which arise under the appeal or are otherwise presented by the information in the case record (for example, the entire episode of care in the appeal), and shall not be limited to addressing the specific issue appealed by a party. In the case of sanctions imposed under Sec. 199.9, the final decision may affirm, increase or reduce the sanction period imposed by CHAMPUS, or otherwise modify or reverse the imposition of the sanction.

32 CFR 199.10(a)(3) Burden of proof. The burden of proof is on the appealing party to establish affirmatively by substantial evidence the appealing party's entitlement under law and this part to the authorization of

Letter Generated: 03/08/17 2:01 PM

CHAMPUS benefits, approval of authorized CHAMPUS provider status, or removal of sanctions imposed under Sec. 199.9 of this part. If a presumption exists under the provisions of this part or information constitutes prima facie evidence under the provisions of this part, the appealing party must produce evidence reasonably sufficient to rebut the presumption or prima facie evidence as part of the appealing party's burden of proof. CHAMPUS shall not pay any part of the cost or fee, including attorney fees, associated with producing or submitting evidence in support of an appeal.

32 CFR 199.21 (k)(3). Prescriptions for pharmaceutical agents for which prior authorization criteria are not met will not be cost-shared under the ▇▇▇▇▇ program.

Discussion

You initially requested coverage for ▇▇▇▇▇ on 02/08/2017. Coverage for this product is available only with prior authorization. When this request was initially reviewed as a factual request, coverage was not authorized because coverage is provided for the diagnoses of heterozygous familial hypercholesterolemia (HeFH), homozygous familial hypercholesterolemia (HoFH), and clinical atherosclerotic cardiovascular disease (ASCVD). Coverage cannot be authorized at this time. Other coverage conditions may apply. ▇▇▇▇ which administers the factual reconsideration process for your ▇▇▇▇ benefit, received your request for reconsideration of this determination on 02/11/2017.

On initial review, it was documented that the beneficiary is being treated for pure hypercholesterolemia, under the care of a cardiologist, lipidologist, or endocrinologist. The review was denied on 02/08/2017 for the reason noted above.

Doctor ▇▇▇▇▇▇▇ has submitted a letter of reconsideration, dated 02/18/2017, indicating the beneficiary is being treated for hyperlipidemia in the setting of statin intolerance and alternative treatment (Lovaza, Zetia)  failure.

Decision

After reconsidering the initial denial and the information provided by you and your physician, we are upholding the initial decision to deny coverage of ▇▇▇▇▇. Specifically, we are unable to overturn the denial because sufficient information has not been provided to establish coverage of the requested medication under the ▇▇▇▇ pharmacy benefit. Specifically, the beneficiary does not have a condition consistent with heterozygous familial hypercholesterolemia (HeFH), homozygous familial hypercholesterolemia (HoFH), and clinical atherosclerotic cardiovascular disease (ASCVD). Coverage is provided for the diagnoses of heterozygous familial hypercholesterolemia (HeFH), homozygous familial hypercholesterolemia (HoFH), and clinical atherosclerotic cardiovascular disease (ASCVD). Additional criteria apply.

The amount of $4,024.05, submitted by ▇▇▇▇▇ on 02/03/2017, is the disputed amount remaining. Because no coverage has ever been provided for this prescription, there will be no recoupment necessary.

Appeal Rights

An appropriate appealing party (i.e., ▇▇▇▇▇ beneficiary), or the appointed representative, has the right to request a formal review. The request must be in writing, be signed, and postmarked or received by:

Letter Generated: 03/08/17 2:01 PM

within 60 calendar days from the date of this decision and must include a copy of this reconsideration determination. For the purposes of ▓▓▓▓, a postmark is a cancellation mark issued by the United States Postal Service. Additional documentation in support of the appeal may be submitted. However, because a request for formal review must be postmarked or received within 60 calendar days from the date of the reconsideration determination, a request for a formal review should not be delayed pending the acquisition of any additional documentation. If additional documentation is to be submitted at a later date, the letter requesting the formal review must include a statement that additional documentation will be submitted and the expected date of submission.

Upon receiving your request, all ▓▓▓▓ pharmacy claims related to the entire course of treatment will be reviewed.

If you have any additional questions, please contact the ▓▓▓▓▓▓▓▓▓▓▓▓▓▓▓▓▓▓▓▓▓▓▓▓.

Respectfully yours,

Department of Defense (DoD) ▓▓▓▓▓▓▓▓▓▓▓▓▓▓
▓▓▓▓▓▓▓▓▓▓▓▓

Appendix Q

Follow-up Letter to Telephone Conversation Upholding Denial, dated June 7, 2017 to Dr. Walter B. Hammond – Page 1

06/07/2017 16:02 FAX ☒002/010

June 7, 2017

Dr. Walter Hammond
5369 Waving Sage Drive
Las Vegas, NV 89149

Dear Dr. Hammond,

This letter is a follow up to your recent telephone conversation with my team member, ███████. We appreciate the time you have taken to inform us of your concerns.

Please accept my sincerest apologies on behalf of ████████████ for the inconvenience you have experienced with obtaining the medication, ███ using your ████████████ Plan.

According to ██ records, Dr. █████ applied for the Prior Authorization (PA) on 02/08/17 (enclosed); however, the request was denied for the following reason: sufficient information had not been provided to establish coverage of the requested medication under the █████ pharmacy benefit. Specifically, the beneficiary does not have a condition consistent with heterozygous familial hypercholesterolemia (HeFH), homozygous familial hypercholesterolemia (HoFH), and clinical atherosclerotic cardiovascular disease (ASCVD). Coverage is provided for the diagnoses of heterozygous familial hypercholesterolemia (HeFH), homozygous familial hypercholesterolemia (HoFH), and clinical atherosclerotic cardiovascular disease (ASCVD). Additional criteria apply. Per the PA Appeal, it has noted that in the absence of ASCVD or baseline LDL-C greater or equal to 190 mg/dL, the committee notes that, at present, ████████ do not have an established role for primary prevention of ASCVD.

On 03/07/17, a reconsideration of the denial was requested; however, the denial was upheld on 03/08/17 (enclosed). The reconsideration denial letter had information concerning your next level of appeal, which was may be sent to:

Director, Appeals, Hearings, and Claims Collection Division

Per the instructions, a beneficiary must appeal within 60 calendar days from the date of the letter and should include a copy of the appeal denial letter; however, at this time ▓ records do not show a second level of appeal has been submitted. Please check with Dr. ▓ Office to inquire if the second level appeal has been processed.

We recognize how important it is to you to have your concerns reviewed in a timely manner. We want you to know that we are committed to addressing your concerns as quickly and efficiently as possible, in order to make your overall experience with ▓ a positive one.

Should you have further questions or concerns, please contact ▓

Again, Dr. Hammond, I apologize for the inconvenience you experienced. ▓ as well as myself, care deeply about our beneficiaries, and are committed to providing you with the excellent service that you should expect.

Sincerely,

cc: Congressman ▓

Enclosure

Appendix R

Second Medical Necessity Letter dated June 9, 2017

Appendix Q

June 9, 2017

Walter Hammond
Case # 3741792

To Whom It May Concern:

I am writing on behalf of my patient, Walter Hammond D.OB 6/2/1930 to document the medical necessity and reconsideration of ▓▓▓▓▓ for the treatment of Pure Hypocholesteremia ASCVD I 25.10. Patient has long history of elevated Cholesterol, Triglycerides, since 2013.

Patient's History and Diagnosis: History of elevated Cholesterol DX Pure hypercholesterolemia and ASCVD patient unable to tolerate statins due to contraindications muscle pain.

Treatment Rationale: Patient has tried and failed other lower lipid lowering agents such as ▓▓▓ and ▓▓▓ ·The use of ▓▓▓ will help to reduce patient's high Cholesterol and Triglycerides. Patient needs ▓▓▓ to help lower Cholesterol and Triglycerides.

Given the patients history, condition and the published data supporting the use of ▓▓▓, I believe the treatment of Walter Hammond with ▓▓▓ is warranted, appropriate and medically necessary.

Denial of this medication will eventually cause the patient to rapidly decline and may result in other health risks.

Your reconsideration in this matter is time sensitive, If you have any questions, I can be reach at ▓▓▓

Sincerely, Dr. ▓▓▓

Appendix S

Copy of letter to Nephrologist Denying Appeal Reconsideration, dated July 11, 2017

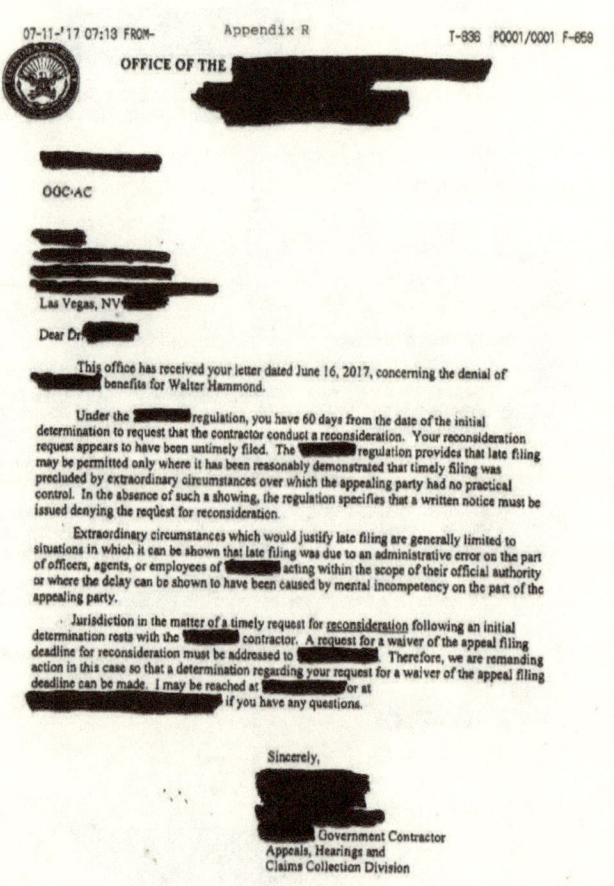

07-11-'17 07:13 FROM-　　　Appendix R　　　T-836　P0001/0001　F-659

OFFICE OF THE ▓▓▓▓▓▓▓▓▓

OGC-AC

Las Vegas, NV ▓

Dear Dr ▓

This office has received your letter dated June 16, 2017, concerning the denial of benefits for Walter Hammond.

Under the ▓▓▓▓▓ regulation, you have 60 days from the date of the initial determination to request that the contractor conduct a reconsideration. Your reconsideration request appears to have been untimely filed. The ▓▓▓▓▓ regulation provides that late filing may be permitted only where it has been reasonably demonstrated that timely filing was precluded by extraordinary circumstances over which the appealing party had no practical control. In the absence of such a showing, the regulation specifies that a written notice must be issued denying the request for reconsideration.

Extraordinary circumstances which would justify late filing are generally limited to situations in which it can be shown that late filing was due to an administrative error on the part of officers, agents, or employees of ▓▓▓▓▓ acting within the scope of their official authority or where the delay can be shown to have been caused by mental incompetency on the part of the appealing party.

Jurisdiction in the matter of a timely request for reconsideration following an initial determination rests with the ▓▓▓▓▓ contractor. A request for a waiver of the appeal filing deadline for reconsideration must be addressed to ▓▓▓▓▓. Therefore, we are remanding action in this case so that a determination regarding your request for a waiver of the appeal filing deadline can be made. I may be reached at ▓▓▓▓▓ or at ▓▓▓▓▓ if you have any questions.

Sincerely,

▓▓▓▓▓
Government Contractor
Appeals, Hearings and
Claims Collection Division

Appendix T

Response to Representative Letter from Department of Defense Requesting Additional Release Form, sent to Dr. Walter B. Hammond, dated August 15, 2017

Appendix S

Operations (J-3)

Dr. Walter B. Hammond
5369 Waving Sage Drive
Las Vegas, NV 89149

AUG 1 5 2017

Dear Dr. Hammond:

This letter is in response to Representative ▓▓▓▓ inquiry on your behalf regarding your ▓▓▓▓ pharmacy benefits. I appreciate the opportunity to address your concerns.

The medication Dr. ▓▓▓▓ requested, ▓▓▓▓, requires a prior authorization. I understand that ▓▓▓▓, denied the prior authorization request on February 9, 2017, and the appeal for reconsideration on March 8, 2017. Because of the specialized nature of this medication, criteria for coverage of its use by a ▓▓▓▓ beneficiary requires that it be prescribed by a cardiologist, lipidologist, or endocrinologist. I have been advised that Dr. ▓▓▓▓ is a nephrologist. I understand that, on July 19, 2017, ▓▓▓▓, an ▓▓▓▓, representative, contacted you to discuss your concerns and inform you of the ▓▓▓▓ criteria for the ▓▓▓▓. If you have any further questions about your prior authorization request or the appeal process, please contact ▓▓▓▓. For all other ▓▓▓▓ pharmacy questions, please contact ▓▓▓▓ at ▓▓▓▓.

The Health Insurance Portability and Accountability Act of 1996 (HIPAA) prohibits me from sharing your protected health information with anyone until I have received from you, a signed Authorization for Disclosure of Medical or Dental Information form—commonly known as a HIPAA release form (DD 2870). While you did provide a signed privacy release to Representative ▓▓▓▓ the Department of Defense is required to use this DD 2870 release form. For all future inquiries regarding ▓▓▓▓ please authorize release of your information from the Military Health System (block 6) to Representative ▓▓▓▓ office (block 6a) when you complete and sign the DD 2870 HIPAA release form. In the absence of a signed HIPPA form, I have informed Representative ▓▓▓▓ that I have responded directly to you. A copy of the DD 2870 form is enclosed for your convenience.

The ▓▓▓▓ is proud to serve our Nation's military heroes and their families and is committed to providing them the best possible health care.

United States Army

Enclosure:
As stated

ABOUT THE AUTHOR

Born in Houston, Texas, Dr. Kennon also lived in northern California and Maryland prior to settling in Las Vegas, Nevada in 1990. She was greatly influenced by her mother (Mrs. Cohuita Price Kennon), maternal grandmother (Mrs. Adah Blanche Price), paternal grandmother (Mrs. Jessie C. Kennon) and aunt (Mrs. Angel Ester Griggsby), all educators and community civic leaders.

After working for 31 years in two states as a School Psychologist and Counselor (kindergarten through college levels), Dr. Kennon entered the entertainment industry in 2012. She started her own business, <u>Sheba Enterprises</u>, and began to broaden her performance skills in the areas of acting and voice over acting.

Dr. Kennon gained broadcast skill experience on radio through her affiliation with several local radio stations where she delivered numerous public service announcements and commercials, and frequently served as show host. In addition to her work in the studio,

Dr. Kennon is recognized for her skills as an audio-book narrator and producer, and as the producer/host of "Possibilities with Dr. Adah Kennon," a weekly hour-long motivational and inspirational radio talk show.

Dr. Kennon holds five advanced degrees in the areas of Psychology, Education and Counseling (BA, 3 Master's Degrees, PhD), and is also a Certified Clinical Mental Health Counselor. She has been recognized in ICE Magazine (Inner Circle Executive Magazine for High Achieving Business Professionals, Continental Who's Who, Autumn 2014) as a Pinnacle Professional, Top Professional Woman. She has been featured in Top 100 Industry Experts in America Magazine (National Association of Distinguished Professionals, Covington Who's Who, First Quarter Edition 2014).

Dr. Kennon has competed in body-building competitions (figure events), appeared as a run-way model for several charity events, and been featured in a body building magazine. She enjoys traveling, gardening and helping her husband, Dr. Walter B. Hammond, with his stress management and self-hypnosis business. She currently assists her husband as his caregiver as he fights his battle with kidney disease and dialysis. Additional information is available at www.247lightheartedcaregivers.com. Dr. Kennon can be contacted via email at: skitldu@gmail.com.

www.ingramcontent.com/pod-product-compliance
Lightning Source LLC
Chambersburg PA
CBHW021406290426
44108CB00010B/413